SEE YA LATER

SEE YA LATER

Arron Crascall

First published in Great Britain in 2017 by Trapeze
an imprint of The Orion Publishing Group Ltd
Carmelite House, 50 Victoria Embankment
London EC4Y 0DZ

An Hachette UK Company

3 5 7 9 10 8 6 4 2

ISBN 978 1 4091 6936 9
ISBN (eBook) 978 1 4091 6939 0
ISBN trade paperback 978 1 4091 6937 6

Typeset by Input Data Services Ltd, Somerset

Printed and bound by CPI Group (UK) Ltd, Croydon CR0 4YY

MIX
Paper from
responsible sources
FSC® C104740

www.orionbooks.co.uk

This book is dedicated to my mum and dad – for just being themselves and for always making me believe in myself!
To my dad for being the bravest and strongest ever!
If I achieve being half the man you are, I'll be a happy man.

CONTENTS

CONTENTS

INTRODUCTION

Three words: See You Later. They are all it took to ruin one man's bum. And do you know what? It was all my fault.

Two years earlier, my worries were no different to anyone else's: work, bills, how I'd get the dirt out of my new Air Maxes, but now I was an internet celebrity and someone had just shown me the first tattoo I'd seen dedicated to me. I was just walking around Dover, minding my own business when this bloke ran up to me screaming my name. He put his shopping down and then – even though the place was packed with people – he dropped his trousers right in the middle of the high street. There in front of me (and about twenty others) was his bare arse, and amongst all the white flesh were those words: See You Later.

'It's See *YA* Later actually, mate,' I said. 'Your tattoo's wrong. I'm really sorry about that.' At this point most people would have dropped to their knees and cried. Not this bloke. He laughed it off.

'Oh well, never mind. I love you, Arron!' Then he did up his jeans and walked off.

That's my kind of person. Not a flasher, I don't have time for flashers. I mean, I like someone who can laugh at any situation and not get caught up in life's everyday stresses (if you consider having your bumcheeks graffitied with utter nonsense one of life's

1

everyday stresses). In fact, so long as you ignore the shockingly hairy crack, he's what I'd call the perfect person. For that reason, I'd like to dedicate my book to him. Here's to you, Ian! Wherever you are, I hope this makes up for all the times you've had to explain your wrongly worded backside to all those potential Mrs Ians.

For legal reasons I've been asked to change Ian's name, so if you're reading this now and thinking 'that's weird, the EXACT SAME THING happened to me, but it couldn't possibly be me because my name's James', then guess what, it is you because so far you're the only bloke who's done that. Oh, and James is a made-up name too, you know.

Protecting the private contents of people's bums is one of many things I've had to learn while writing my book, and yes, you heard me right: my book. An actual book! I'm writing a real-life proper book!!!! Please forgive the excitement, but this is a huge deal for me. A massive opportunity that's only possible thanks to the incredible amount of support I've received not just from my family and friends but you lot, too. In fact, especially you lot too. Over the years I've received an overwhelming amount of love from the people that watch my videos (and not just Ian); people saying I make their day or cheer them up when they're feeling down. And I'm just a fat bloke in skinny jeans dancing around in a supermarket! Well, let me tell you, if you're one of those people who gets a bit of joy from what I do, then please know that it's nothing compared to the feeling I get after I press that upload button. Every single one of the likes (and Hahas and Loves and Wows) you send my way hits me like an enormous jolt of positive electricity, and for that I will always be extremely grateful. For the record, this is a metaphor, I'm not actually hooked up to a machine that electrocutes me every time you press Like. That would be insane. It only shocks me when you press the Angry button.

Seriously, though, I can't believe I'm about to follow in the footsteps of some of my favourite writers: J.K. Rowling, Roald Dahl, William Shakespeare and the genius behind the Goosebumps books, Mr R.L. Stine. I hope I can channel a little bit of what I've learned by reading their books (and by reading, I mean scanning the blurb on the back and maybe the first and last chapters). In fact, I'd say the most important thing I've learned is that in order to be taken seriously as a writer, I need a fancy initialled name. R.L. Stine? J.K. Rowling? J.R. Hartley? Say goodbye to Arron Crascall and say hello to A.R. Crascall (Robert, since you ask). Actually, scratch that. Say hello to B.A. Crascall, after my childhood hero B.A. Baracus. No, you know what? Forget B.A., forget A.R., I've got it. This, my first-ever book, shall be written by my official writer's name, chosen after my one true love . . . K.F.C. Crascall.

Not that this is the first time K.F.C. Crascall has ever put his thoughts into words. On Facebook alone I've already written enough to create my own *Game of Thrones* – that is, if *Game of Thrones* had fewer dragons and more sunglasses emojis. Hang on, where are my emojis? What do you mean, books don't have emojis?? Looks like old Nokia 3310-style crying-face emojis are coming. :'-(:'-(:'-(Seriously, though, take away my emojis, you take away my power. It's like taking away Harry Potter's wand, stealing all of Shakespeare's biros or cutting off Van Gogh's ear. This is going to be tough, I won't lie. I genuinely think that emojis are an advancement in the way we talk with each other. Well, not talk, I've never met someone that can actually speak emoji, but written down, they're the best way to communicate – a picture tells a thousand words, right? In the future we'll cut down on paper as all books will be written in emoji. I hear they're making an emoji movie, so it's only a matter of time, surely? And they'd be a lot quicker to read, too. *A Midsummer Night's Dream* would go: moon emoji, girl emoji, boy emoji, heart emoji, donkey emoji. *Of Mice and Men* would go: man emoji, hand emoji, mouse emoji, skull emoji. *Jurassic Park* would be tough as there's no dinosaur emoji, so I guess crocodiles would have to do on that one.

Before we get any further, here's a rundown of my top five emojis.

1) Sunglasses emoji (Of course. See ya later!)
2) Cry-laughing emoji (I always need at least two of these on all my posts)
3) Shy monkey emoji (I won't tell you what I've received to make me post those shy monkeys!)
4) Cheeky emoji (As in cheeky Nando's. Love a cheeky Nando's)
5) Heart emoji (Love to Char and my kids! – and to you too, reading this)

So what is this book? And why am I writing it now? Well, consider it my way of spreading some much-needed positivity at a time when the world is frankly a little bit pants. There are enough stresses in life without the hundreds of news stories that come out every week that rile people up even more. We are a world divided, and it's up to yours truly to save it! Okay, I'm not going to save it, but if by reading this then you find life even the slightest bit better, then I'll consider it a job well done.

Which isn't to say there's nothing that rubs me up the wrong way. You'll see when you read on that I have my bugbears (I'm looking at you, food bloggers!), but at the end of the day it's all about looking for that silver lining. Like most people in Britain, I'm a firm believer in making the most out of a bad situation. If a plane crash-landed on a desert island, while everyone sees doom, I'd be with all the other Brits jumping for joy at the prospect of a free beach holiday. What else would you expect from the nation that every winter prays for a crippling blizzard just so we can have a free snow day? You and I could be trapped in a cave right now, cornered by a hangry[1] bear, it's razor-sharp teeth bearing down on us. The beast would let out this fearsome, almighty growl that would be loud enough to cause the bones inside us to rattle, but rather than wet ourselves in horror, because we're British I'm probably more likely to whisper in your ear, 'Doesn't this bear look a bit like Donald Trump?' And after reading this book, rather than yelling, 'What the hell are you talking about Arron, that bear is literally about to rip your bloody head off!?', you'll reply, 'Totally. Shall we try and get a selfie with him?'

I'm here to remind you that when life gives you lemons, make lemonade. No, in fact, when life gives you lemons, make a fool out of yourself in the lemonade aisle. Actually don't do exactly that, that's my thing. Oh and by the way, talking of Donald Trump, if you want to hear my thoughts on the Trump-meister general, you can flick straight ahead to page 129 where I have an entire chapter dedicated to him.

This book is my take on the world. The things that are important to me. The good, the bad and the stupid (there's a lot of this third one). You'll find stories about my past, a lot of views on the present and some opinions on how to make the future a more enjoyable place. It's part biography, part self-help book, part textbook, part travel book (well, Dover at least); you'll find comedy, crime, drama and of course a little bit of romance (if your idea of romantic is staring at a girl for a whole year through a playground fence).[2] In fact, I want to put so much into this book, you won't just see it in

---

1 Hangry, as in hungry and angry. It's something I'm known to suffer from a lot. Especially when after half an hour waiting in a fancy restaurant (who am I kidding, it's Nando's again), that waitress finally comes over to deliver your food and you're brought to tears when you realise it was never yours and she gives it to some annoying kid behind you.

2 Relax! We were both schoolkids, you weirdo.

every bookshop in the country, you'll see it on every shelf in every bookshop in the country.

And where is this book now? Yes, this is the book you're currently holding in your hands. If it's still in the bookshop and you're just reading to get a taste before you decide to buy it, then a) go ahead and take it to the till, what have you got to lose? and b) we're already six pages in – how has security let you get away with reading so much before telling you to jog on? Madness. Perhaps this book is far away from the high street. Perhaps it left the bookshop long ago and has found its way to that most precious of homes. A place all authors long to find their work. A place of peace, tranquillity and discarded cardboard tubes you refuse to be the one to chuck away. I'm talking about your toilet.

Thank you for inviting me into such sacred territory. A person's toilet is their most treasured location and I'm grateful for you inviting me inside (just make sure you wash your hands thoroughly after you're done wiping). Do you currently have those red marks on the tops of your legs? Are you completely numb from the thighs down? If not, then settle in and keep reading. But if you are, and you're already showing signs of leg numbness, then you'll know from experience that as soon as you try and stand up, you're going to be hit with a million volts of pins and needles, forcing you to hit the deck a whimpering, quivering wreck, the pain will be so intense you'll wish you'd stuck to reading something shorter like the back of that Herbal Essences bottle you've already read a thousand times instead. So you know what? You might as well just sit back, put your phone on silent, ignore the queue of people outside ordering you to get a move on and carry on reading my book, because we're only just getting started.

Welcome to the world according to Arron Crascall.

Oh, and before I forget . . . SEE YA LATER! (Well, on the next page, at least).

CHAPTER ONE

ARRON WHO?

I just realised some of you might not have a clue who I am. Maybe you got given this book by a friend. Maybe you don't have the internet. Maybe you're one of those people that still has a house phone. If for these or any other reason you've never heard the name Arron Crascall, then here's a little chapter about me.

I'm the bloke that keeps appearing on your Facebook. Open it up and you won't have to look far to find me dancing with strangers in Trafalgar Square or blasting out some Mariah in a supermarket (shout out to Bridge Street Morrisons!). Facebook says I'm an Entertainer, but if you actually watch my videos you'll realise I'm more like a professional idiot.

Seriously, I'm sure everyone's first reaction to seeing me is 'What a plum', and if you saw me in person you'd definitely think that. Catch me in the street and you'll likely find me with my arm stretched out, phone in the air, shouting into the camera lens. It's not a good look. But public humiliation is something that's worth enduring when you know it's going to get a load of people giggling. Yes, that's exactly the excuse all class clowns in school use, so it may come as a shock for newbies to learn that I'm actually thirty-four. Well, a thirty-four-year-old child.

Having said that, I'm thirty-four *now*. You could be reading this ten years from now and I'll be forty-four. Maybe it's thirty years from now, and you've dug this out in some remote car boot sale. In which case I'm sixty-four. No doubt I'll still be out and about with my phone in the air doing some live Sunday See Ya Laters with you guys, squeezing my saggy old pins into the same pair of skinnies. But maybe it's even further into the future than that. Maybe this is 100 years from now and the teachings of Arron Crascall have become the school syllabus. A generation of kids being taught how to bob their heads forward just right so that their Ray-Bans fall perfectly onto their noses. The school uniform would be Air Maxes and spray-on jeans, and the school motto would be 'Post Ya Videre' (take a guess what that's Latin for – thank you Google Translate!).

Having said all that, Char is in my ear as we speak asking what I want to do for my thirty-fifth birthday. It's only a week away, which means by the time this book is out all the numbers above are wrong. Sorry about that.

Who's Char? Charlotte is my beautiful girlfriend. She's the person I owe my entire world to and that's no exaggeration. We've been together since long before my ugly face was on the cover of a book. Back when I met her I was working behind the bar on the ferries for P&O, which sounds a lot more glamorous than it was. Seriously, it was horrible having to watch people come and go, enjoying their holidays, while I was trapped travelling back and forth between the same two ports. It was like *Groundhog Day*, only with more drunken stags and screaming children.

You'll notice from all the times Char pops up in my videos that she is infinitely better-looking than me. Even the totally unimpressed face she pulls after I try and impress her with my Chewbacca impression for the millionth time is adorable. Poor Char. You know there's even a group of people online who every time she appears in one of my videos tweet their support for her having to put up with an idiot like me and the idiot things I do? They rock the name #teamcharlotte, but let me tell you no one is more #teamcharlotte than me.

I am living proof that it's worth trying to punch above your weight and if you're persistent enough, even fat boys can bag themselves a total babe. Charlotte does an amazing job at keeping me level-headed. She doesn't let success go to my head and will be the first person to tell me if something isn't funny. I won't post anything without getting her opinion first. Doing this for a living (whatever *this* is) is a massive blast, but it's nothing compared to the fun I have at home mucking about with Char and the kids. Which is the other important thing: Charlotte is an incredible mum. And she needs to be when yours truly is by far the biggest child in the house.

Which brings me on to my kids: Alfie, Mia and Evie. They are the reason I get up in the morning, and I'm not just talking about having to sort out their breakfast and put *Frozen* on for the first of fifteen times that day. If there are any other parents out there that have accidentally stepped on a Lego brick in their bare feet, you'll know not a day goes by when you're not cursing their names, but one look into their eyes and you soon realise they're the most important things in the world. Is it okay to call them things? Oh well, I've said it now. The scariest thing, though, is when your children start to behave just like you. My eldest, Alfie, is already massively into his *Star Wars*. I swear it's like I'm talking to my past self sometimes.

If I had the chance to, there'd be loads I'd want to tell my younger self. Mainly it would be 'Stop stuffing your face with so much food', but then again, if I wasn't a chubby teen, I wouldn't have had to work so hard being funny to get people to like me and then where would I be today? Back on the ferries, probably. The only thing I'd be filming on my phone would be a passenger drunkenly trying to impress his mates dancing on a table before we hit a wave and he's sent flying to the other end of the ship. Mind you, might get a few views, that one.

And that's pretty much me in a nutshell. There's plenty more: my mum, my dad, my Dover, but hey, we're just getting started and we've got an entire book ahead of us. It's a marathon, not a sprint after all (I say that like I've got any experience marathoning or sprinting). Right, on to the next chapter. See Ya Later!

I've been told by the people that publish the book I can't end every chapter with See Ya Later. Sorry about that. Don't blame me, blame Anna.

CHAPTER TWO

SKINNY JEANS

Okay, let's get the biggest topic in early: my skinny jeans. This is probably the thing I get asked about more than any other subject. And why not? They're important to me, and dare I say it a vital part of modern society. In fact, I reckon skinny jeans could well be the most significant fashion development since Eve said to Adam, 'You know, I can still see your junk behind that dock leaf?'

But I've not always felt that way. Twenty years ago if you'd told me I'd be an ambassador for skintight legwear I would have laughed in your face and ripped the poppers from your Adidas tracksuit bottoms.

Sorry, total diversion here but can we take a moment to remember the Adidas popper tracksuit bottom? What a masterpiece in design that was. If you're too young to know what I'm talking about, they were basically like any ordinary pair of tracksuit bottoms except they had poppers lined all the way up the side, which meant one swift tug and they completely fell apart. Adidas essentially managed to turn every teenager in the country into a qualified stripper. It was great, but let your guard down for one second on non-uniform day and you risked having your bare white pins exposed to the entire school. Which, if you were me, would not have been a good look.

Right, back to the skinnies and yes, if the younger me was here right now, he would be logging on to Facebook just to join the million other people online who like to tell me on a regular basis that I'm too big to pull them off. Well if any of you naysayers are reading this right now, I've got one thing to make clear: pulling them off is the easy part – you should try putting them on.

Arron Crascall's guide to getting into skinny jeans

REMEMBER: take your time. This is not a race, it is an art form and like all art it requires significant levels of patience.

1) Prepare your legs so they are ready to receive the jeans. That means making sure all surfaces are clean and, crucially, completely dry. Don't you dare try putting them on soon after a shower. If you want to have any chance of this epic task working, you've got to get those things dry as a bone first.
2) Shaving/waxing your legs is not necessary, but do make sure to rein in any particularly long hairs – believe me, you don't want any unwanted snags.
3) Roll up each trouser leg as tightly as possible. They should each resemble a sort of denim doughnut.
4) DO NOT EAT YOUR TROUSER LEGS, NO MATTER HOW MUCH THEY RESEMBLE DOUGHNUTS.
5) Slide each foot through the corresponding 'doughnut', ensuring they are completely through before attempting step 6.
6) Unroll the doughnuts, one at a time, letting the jeans apply themselves onto the full length of your legs.

7) The above step will start easy but completely fail you before you even reach the knee, so start pulling like you've never pulled before.

8) You're not pulling hard enough! Put some effort into it!

9) Seriously, bounce around the room like an idiot if you have to or lie with your feet in the air and let gravity help.

10) Done it! Congratulations! Now you're ready to start your day! And by the way, don't even think about trying to adjust your meat and two veg. They are where they are and that's where they're going to stay. Unless you want to start again from step 3? No, didn't think so.

A final warning about aftercare: Do not, under any circumstances, ever wash your skinny jeans as you won't be able to handle any unnecessary shrinkage. The safe thing to do is spray with deodorant until all unwanted smells have gone. Considering the amount the average man sweats in skinny jeans, I reckon about half a can will do.

If you haven't worn them, you're missing out. It's like receiving a billion hugs all at once just on your legs. Although if you're also slightly on the large size you shouldn't wear a skinny top at the same time – our bodies aren't equipped to receive so much affection all at once. When I wear skinny jeans they squeeze my leg flab all the way up towards my waist like a tube of toothpaste. If I was wearing a skinny top too, it would be pushing the flesh from my top half down. The two forces combined would create the biggest muffin top the world has ever seen. In fact, forget the muffin, I'd look like Saturn!

The skinny jean revolution isn't going anywhere either, so don't bother fighting it. Within ten years I'm sure every man will be wearing a pair. In fact, we'll probably be on to something else by then, and at the rate we keep stealing clothes from women, us blokes might well be running around in boob tubes before you know it.

If you're a girl reading this and your fella is still walking around in boot-cut jeans, do the world a favour and burn them. You should not be subjected to such a horrific sight, and neither should anyone else. Unless of course your boyfriend is Chuck Norris. He is the only man that is entitled to rock a boot cut. And I'm not just saying that because if I don't he'll find me and roundhouse-kick my head clean off.

You ever think about what we might be wearing in the future? I for one hope somebody finally invents a hat guaranteed not to give you hat hair, or a truly self-ironing shirt or, with a bit of luck, beaded jewellery you can buy on holiday that doesn't make you look like an absolute plonker the second you arrive back in the UK.

Some fashions are timeless, though. I might as well have been born in Nike Air Maxes, they've been attached to my feet for so long. They're one of many things you can't believe are as popular now as they were in the '90s: like Take That. At my funeral the vicar will no doubt say, 'Arron died doing what he loved: wearing a sweet pair of Air Max 90s. Now all rise for "Never Forget".'

Then there's the Ray-Bans, another timeless piece of fashion item and an integral part of my day-to-day get-up (and work uniform, let's be honest). No one can argue that Wayfarers are the undisputed kings of eyewear. What else could compete with them? Aviators come and go but will never again be '*Top Gun* cool'; those futuristic-looking Oakleys are only ever worn by either extreme snowboarders or county cricketers, and while all of us went

14

through a very short phase of wearing those weird little circular John Lennon numbers, I don't think even old John would have said he looked good in them. No, the Wayfarers will be around forever. They still look as good now as they did in *Risky Business* in 1983 – even if Tom Cruise doesn't. (Just kidding, Tom, you look great – now, while you're here, how about a role in the next *Mission Impossible*?).

Another reason they're the greatest sunglasses you can buy is they have the perfect weight to them for performing the Arron Crascall-patented See Ya Later. Try doing it with a pair of cheap knock-offs and you're asking for trouble. Believe me, there are few things worse than bowling up to someone in public, having everything go right: the perfect punter, the perfect reaction, the perfect line, only for the glasses not to drop from your noggin. You think I look like an idiot when it goes right? You should see me when it goes wrong.

By the way, if you're one of those people who has still never seen any of my videos (go online now – this is your final warning) then you probably don't have a clue what a 'See Ya Later' is. Sorry about that, I've been banging on about them loads already. Like I said, if you're yet to see one, go online and check one out now, mate. But if you can't get online (maybe you're underground, in a plane or your phone's stuck on that BT-FON thing, whatever that is) then I'll do my best to try and describe it to you.

'See Ya Later' is one of my longest-running hits. It's also my personal favourite, and judging by some of your reactions online it strikes a chord with you lot too. It may look easy to do, but there's a lot going on that makes them pretty tricky to pull off. The most important thing is probably the sunglasses, which are perfectly perched on top of my head before I begin. With the shades set, I find someone who I think would be up for a laugh, sneak up behind them and whisper 'Psst!' in their ear. A lot of the time I get rumbled before I even get to this point; I mean, look at the size of me, I'm not exactly built for sneaking! So I whisper in their ear and they turn round, usually with a look of shock and confusion on their face. I then give them a useful piece of advice like, 'It's gonna rain later, better grab a brolly', or 'Buy the tulips, they come out lovely this time of year', before rocking my head forward, causing the Ray-Bans to fall perfectly on to my nose. I then declare 'See Ya Later!' and march off with the sort of swagger more suitable for a bloke that's just won a hundred quid on all three of his scratch cards.

If I come up to you in the street and I try a hit but it goes wrong, you're very welcome to take the mick. I love it really, and over the years I've grown very used to it. But my favourite jokes I get from the public are always about my jeans. (Yes, we're back to the jeans – seriously, I could talk about them this entire book if I had to). My, oh my do people like to tell me I'm too big for them, and how I shouldn't be wearing them. I like to picture the rage in their eyes when they see me on their smartphones, gyrating away after someone's taken the hand of dance (that's another one of my videos. Seriously, am I going to have to explain all of my videos?). Ninety per cent of the time it's all jokes, of course. That's why I love my followers so much even when it gets nasty you know it's all banter, just like it is with friends I've known my whole life.

In fact, here's a few of my favourite messages I've received over the years. All for your enjoyment.

'I've seen more meat on a sparrow's kneecap!' – Tom
'My sister called, she wants her skinny jeans back' – Jenn
'Your skinny jeans deserve a channel of their own' – Ed
'That Arron Crascall kid looks like Dr Eggman in them skinny jeans with his pot belly' – Jake

'How does he even get them jeans on?' – Emma (Well lucky for you, Emma, I've already written a whole section explaining exactly that).

Sorry to go all Springer's Final Thought before we've even reached the third chapter, but as a man used to getting a lot of stick, I thought I should pass on some advice to any people who may be in a similar position. So if you're on the receiving end of haters, whether like me it's because you have a soft spot for stretchy denim, or maybe it's something else about the clothes you wear, or maybe it's the way you talk or the way you walk or the way you write 'your' when everyone tells you you should be writing 'you're', my advice is not to take yourself so seriously. If you can have a laugh about your own imperfections, then no one else can. You own it. It's yours. Now obviously it's my job to make myself a laughing stock, but once upon a time I used to be sensitive about things like my weight and stuff. Then as soon as *I* became the first one to crack the jokes, it took all the ammo away from the haters. So yeah, that's it, don't take yourself so seriously.

Speaking of which, in the next chapter prepare to hear some pretty embarrassing things about me. Remember Ian from the start of the book? The bloke with 'See You Later' tattooed on his bumcheek? Well now it's time to talk about *my* tattoos – and I'm not just talking about the ones you can see with my clothes on.

CHAPTER THREE

TATTOOS

There are two types of people in this world. There's the people who watch *Tattoo Fixers* on E4 and go, 'How on earth could anyone be so stupid as to get *that* drawn on them for the rest of their life?' Then there's the people who watch the exact same thing and go, 'Poor bastard, I know what that feels like.'

I bet there's a lot more of us out there in the second group than you think, and yes, that's right mate, I said 'us'; I've got some stupid tattoos, but do you know what? I wouldn't change a single one of them. They are literally part of me, and if they raise a bit of a laugh when people see them well, hey, what could be more appropriate?

Let's start with a big one then. I'm going to hold my hands up here and admit something . . . I have a rather embarrassing tattoo most commonly referred to as a 'tramp stamp'. It's not something I admit to very often, but I think it's only fair that you know. In fact, I'm tired of keeping it a secret; everyone should know. You can't see me but I'm currently in the pub on my laptop typing this, and I'm shouting it to the rooftops like a dramatic confession. MY NAME IS ARRON CRASCALL AND I HAVE A TRAMP STAMP! Wow, it feels good to admit that. Not for the poor lady on the table next to me, though; I think I've exploded her eardrums.

For those who aren't tat savvy, here's what a tramp stamp is: it's a tattoo positioned on the lower back, just above one's bum crack. I don't mean to offend any of my tramp-stamp brothers and sisters (mostly sisters) when I say it is typically associated with quite 'promiscuous' (*cough* slutty! *cough*) women. Search on the internet and Wikipedia will tell you it's . . .

. . . a tattoo popular amongst some women in the 2000s which gained a reputation for its feminine appeal. They are sometimes accentuated by low-rise jeans and crop tops, and are considered erotic by some.'

In other words, not a tattoo typically found on dudes like me. Not that it's an unpopular thing to have; celebrities sporting tramp stamps include classy ladies like Britney Spears, Lindsay Lohan and Tulisa, so you can't argue I'm in very sophisticated company. Tulisa in particular is queen of the tramp stamps. She actually has the coveted 'tramp-stamp double', which is an incredible sight. In the traditional position, above the bottom, she has her own awesome poem that if you google her[3] you'll find reads like this:

She is strong when she is weak
She is brave when she is scared
She is humble when she is victorious

I think we can all agree this is a thing of beauty. Three short sentences that send a powerful message to women all over the world, making Tulisa Contostavlos a monument to feminism and a role model to women everywhere. Seriously, mate, I think I might etch that into my daughters' bunk beds or something, it's that

---

3 Please take care when googling Tulisa; there are videos on there that once you see, you can't *unsee*.

inspirational. But then you scroll further down Google Images.[4] You see, on her front side she has another tattoo that is positioned just above her 'you-know-what'. It's a crudely drawn four-leaf clover with a slightly less inspiring message that reads: 'Lucky you'. Needless to say I won't be etching *that* one onto my daughters' bunk beds.

Believe it or not, I'm not the only *man* out there with a tramp stamp. One bloke in particular is actually one of the most beautiful men on the planet and famous for having some of the best tattoos going. It's only David bloomin' Beckham! Yes, David Beckham has a bloody slag tag. You'd think a guy like David could make anything look cool, right? Not when you consider his tramp stamp is his son's name, 'Brooklyn'.

In fact, you know they say he's called Brooklyn because that's where he was conceived? Well, maybe the tat isn't Brooklyn as in 'my son, Brooklyn'; maybe instead it's just a reminder of 'the night I done it with a Spice Girl' – which, let's be honest, we'd all have done if we could. So far my wildest night of sex took place on holiday in Wales, but as tattoos go, 'Newport Caravan Park' doesn't quite have the same punch, does it?

Is it just me that thinks it's a little bit weird to have your son's name tattooed in that spot? If you think it's perfectly fine and ordinary, then good for you, you're great and I'm a horrible person. But here's a little exercise that might change your opinion, and I'm sorry, I don't think you're going to like it.

Picture your name written out in some really fancy letters. I'm talking ornate, gothic-looking ones. Like the kind monks like to start their chapters with. See it written out in front of you. Looks

---

4 Again, please take care, someone might have even posted a screengrab of the video. Make sure you have Safe Search on, is all I'm saying. This is your final NSFW warning.

good, doesn't it? You can tell a lot of effort has gone into each letter and how they flow into each other. Maybe you've got some thorny vines worked in with the name, adding even more detail as they wrap beautifully around each letter and transform your simple, ordinary name into a wild, overgrown natural beauty. The vines are full of sharp thorns, and at the end of each vine is an impressively realistic rose. This isn't just your name, this is something special. What you are looking at is art. No, more than that, this is something you might find in a posh gallery or museum. What you are looking at is a masterpiece. Then, just two inches below that masterpiece, picture your dad's dirty, sweaty, stinking bum crack. Not exactly the *Mona Lisa* any more, is it? No, it's absolutely awful. Sorry about that, guys, I told you you weren't going to like it!

Speaking of bums and roses (surely someone's got to form a cover band with that name), my all-time favourite celebrity tattoo belongs to Ms Cheryl Cole. No, wait, belongs to Ms Cheryl Fernandez-Versini. No, that's still not right. Has she gone back to being called Cheryl Tweedy? Of course not – it's Cheryl Payne. Hang on, they're not married, are they? God, this is difficult. Hang on, let me start again.

Speaking of bums and roses (how you getting on with that cover band?), my all-time favourite celebrity tattoo belongs to the girl from Girls Aloud that used to be married to a footballer but now has a baby with Liam off One Direction. Phew, nailed it. As I was saying, my favourite celeb tattoo might be one you already know about, but for those of you that don't, Cheryl has her entire bum covered in roses. Her *entire* bum. It's an incredible sight, and a long way to go to try and mask the impact of your farts. Apparently it took three days and cost as much as a car. I reckon if they attempted to cover my entire bum in roses, it would take a week instead and probably cost the same as a minibus.

Back to my tramp stamp, though, and I'm sorry to say that the location of the tattoo on my body isn't the only thing that's embarrassing about it. It's also what's written. And before you start assuming it's my son's name, no it's not. At least then I could get some amount of respect by saying it was a loving tribute. No, I'm afraid what's written on my lower back is much worse than that. The name on my tramp stamp, is *my* name.

Who gets their own name tattooed on them?? What kind of self-obsessed egomaniac does that? I hear what you're saying, 'Probably the same type of bloke that videos himself every day of the week for a living, Arron!' And of all the places, this is in that coveted just-above-the-bum spot. Look at it this way: the devotion I have towards myself is the exact same amount that David Beckham has towards his first born child. That's not good, is it?

Although what if I told you it wasn't *quite* my name? Let me explain. I'm not saying whoever did my tattoo accidentally misspelled Arron (he wouldn't be the first – it's not Aaron, okay!) but if I were to show you it, you probably wouldn't immediately think it says Arron. You see, the tattoo of my name above my bum looks like 'Akkon' instead.

AKKON? Who the hell is Akkon? Absolutely nobody, that's who. Thanks to the extra K, I can't even get away with claiming it's in honour of rapper-slash-bendy-voice-supremo Akon. I'm stuck with absolute jargon on there permanently, and it's all down to an out-of-control ego and a terrible choice of font.

Are tattoos a waste of money?

It really annoys me when I hear old people say tattoos are a waste of money. You don't hear me judging them for keeping a cabinet full of china plates no one uses, do you?

The first tattoo I ever got was a small black sun in the middle of my right forearm. The story of getting that done is probably the same as most people's first tattoo; I snuck out of school with a friend and lied about my age. I was only fifteen and convinced the man in charge that I was twenty. I don't know why I went so high, I only had to be eigheen and besides, the fact that I was wearing a school uniform was a definite sign I was lying. Perhaps he took pity on this tragic-looking kid and thought, 'I don't care how old he is, this young lad is going to need all the help he can get in life, and if breaking the law will give him just a little bit of hope towards some credibility when he gets back to school, then so be it.' Although I'd bet any money he just took one look at me and thought, 'This is going to be the easiest fifty quid I make all week.'

That day I was in there alongside my good friend Craig. We left the place with the same identical small black sun. Even now, after all this time we still greet each other the same way we did twenty years ago by throwing our forearms in the air and touching suns. If you saw us doing it and you didn't know about the matching tattoos, you'd assume we were just really terrible at high fives.

The guy who ended up doing our tattoos was this junior tattooist by the name of Sean Sparks (cool name, right? Sounds like a super hero). At the time this was also Sean's first-ever tattoo, which I think makes that one the bravest ink I've ever had done. Me and Sean are now really close mates, and I wouldn't dare go to anyone else for some work. He's an absolute artist. If you ever decide to get a tattoo yourself then I suggest you make the trip to Dover to see my man Sean!

It's a big decision, getting a tattoo, and like most people there's plenty of designs I've thought about getting but then decided against (thank God). Here's some of the most ridiculous ones that have crossed my mind over the years.

1) 18

You know when you watch a movie and it says how old you have to be to watch it? I used to want that 18 logo on my shoulder. I can't remember if it was to celebrate turning eighteen or to say, 'Watch out, this guy's as dangerous as an 18 film', but both were terrible reasons.

2) My face

One late night with a friend we got to thinking about ageing and how tattoos look as you get older. Well, we thought wouldn't it be fun to get tattoos of our faces and see if they age better or worse than our actual faces. It's an interesting experiment, if only to prove how long a man can survive while being totally repulsive to women.

3) Textbook

This was the dream, right? Who needs to revise when you can have the answers tattooed on your body? No, I never would have done this but I did like the idea of having an excerpt from my favourite book written on me. The problem is when all you've read is *FHM* and the blurb on the back of *To Kill A Mockingbird*, your options are limited. But don't let that stop you. If you want to go ahead and get one of the pages of my book tattooed on your back, then be my guest – send me the picture and I promise to reply!

4) You-know-what ;-)

What man into his inking hasn't at one stage thought about getting something drawn onto his tackle? I'll admit this one was always going to be a long shot, but once upon a time it did cross my mind. If you think about it, we're talking about the original dick-pics here. It would be worth it just to take a photo of it and send it to someone special. It would be a dick-pic dick-pic. Like a way sexier version of the movie *Inception*.

You'll notice looking at the cover of this book that my arms are entirely sleeved up. I like to think of them as a little tribute to my family. Across my wrists it reads 'Family Forever' – one word at the end of each arm. Also on my wrists I have two little love hearts: one with the letter C dedicated to my gorgeous Charlotte, and another with the number three in Roman numerals as a tribute to my three kids.

If you're thinking, 'But Arron, what if you have more kids?' Well, to be honest, I think I'm out – three is enough for me! In fact, me and my mates were saying one of these days we should have a 'Vasectomy Day'. It's sort of like a stag do, except you and your mates meet up at hospital, get the snip together, then by lunchtime you're hitting the pubs for an all-day bender to celebrate cutting off your baby batter. And if through some miracle I do end up with a fourth kid or a fifth, a sixth or even more, then because the 'three' on my wrist is in Roman numerals, I'll just turn it into a tally, like a prisoner counting the years he's been in prison. (Not that I reckon parenthood is anything like a prison sentence, I promise!)

I think it's important that your tattoos reflect what's important to you, and there isn't anything bigger in my life than Char and the kids. The single biggest tattoo on my body you won't find looking at the cover of this book. It's a poem dedicated to my boy Alfie, and it runs the full length of my torso from my armpit to my waist. It's written in this beautiful italic font, and if anyone catches a glimpse of it, it always gets a lot of attention. Needless to say, it looks impressive and I'm very proud of it.

There was a very low point in my life when I had this done, during which it felt like the only decent thing I had going for me was this gorgeous little boy that I was proud to call my son. It's the way I feel now about all my kids, but at that time he was all I had and I felt compelled to do something special, so I searched long and hard on the internet to find the words that captured what I was feeling before enduring three and a half hours of pain and discomfort at the mercy of the needle. Everything is much better now, of course, and the tattoo serves as a pretty effective reminder that when the world isn't going my way, I shouldn't get too hung up on the things I'm powerless to control, and instead I should surround myself with and appreciate the good things in life, like my kids. I just wish I had a better canvas for my tribute. Whatever you say about the sentiment of the poem, the sagging side of the average man in his mid-thirties is not exactly the most flattering of places to pick for your loving tributes. I swear, when I lean to pick up the kids' toys or put on my shoes or move in pretty much any way, my body contorts and that poem looks totally different. It could be the world's first-ever tattooed moving image. Or better yet, the first-ever tattooed gif.

And my God, did this one hurt. It hurt more than any other tattoo I've had before or since. Normally when a tattooist sees you're hurting, they give you this mouth guard to bite on. Only on this occasion they didn't have any lying around, so instead they gave me one of those cardboard tubes you get inside toilet roll. Here I am going through the biggest physical pain of my life, and the only thing I have to combat it is a piece of card that's been living next to the crapper!

So I'm lying there, gritting my teeth on a poo-infested cardboard tube, knowing the pain will be worth it because each word of this poem represents how I feel about my boy. And the guy with the needle starts writing . . .

Life, grant me the serenity to accept the things I cannot change.

Yep, I really believe that. There's no point crying over spilt milk.

The courage to change the things I can.

26

That too. Although courage is something I'm not short of, actually. You need plenty of balls to run up to a random skinhead and ask him to dance with you.

And the wisdom to know the difference.

And more importantly, the wisdom to triple-check every tattoo I ever get done, because for those of you who haven't already realised, the poem I had branded onto my body for all eternity was in fact the official poem for Alcoholics Anonymous.

Now, I have got nothing but admiration for the incredible work that gets done within support groups, and of course the utmost respect for the struggle of alcoholism. I am fortunate to have never suffered from it, but knowing people who have, it's something I take very seriously. However, as a man who is rarely caught without a beer in his hand, having the wise words of Alcoholics Anonymous tattooed all over your body can be a particularly difficult thing to explain. Especially when you're on holiday, topless and dual-fisting a pint of lager and a Pina Colada.

CHAPTER FOUR

CLEAN EATING

That's right, my body is a shrine, a totem of the love I have for my friends, family and some bloke called Akkon, whoever he is. My body is sacred and therefore I treat it like a temple. Well, err, no, not exactly. Food is great and I can't get enough of it, that's the truth of it.

I'm not one of those people that has avocado for breakfast, lunch and dinner, and I'm certainly not one of those people who starts their day with a green juice. If kale was as tasty to drink as people claim, then why don't they make Kale Coke? I'll tell you why – because kale tastes like feet.

Where did kale even come from? I swear it didn't exist a few years ago. Well, I did a bit of searching and read online that apparently only a few years ago, the world's biggest user of kale was Pizza Hut, and they only used it to decorate the salad bar – they didn't even feed it to their customers! And all of a sudden, now it's considered a superfood, whatever the hell that means (I'm pretty sure it's not an aubergine in a cape). Everyone says you need more superfoods in your diet, well, let me tell you, if they're all as bad as kale then you can count me out. Superfoods shouldn't be about how many vitamins or antioxidants they've got inside them. It's simple: superfoods should be foods that taste super. So put away your spirulina! If you're looking for a happy, fulfilling and less pretentious diet, get this lot down your neck.

1) Sweet and Sour Sauce

Add this to anything and you're on to a winner. Hell, you could even put it on kale and you'd have a tasty meal on your hands. My personal favourite is ordering a Big Mac and pouring some of the old SAS in there. Beautiful. Try it and I promise you won't have it any other way.

2) Pot Noodle

Peel off the lid and what you see inside looks like a barren wasteland. In this state it looks like someone walked around with a plastic pot in their hands and picked up any old crap they found on the floor. Yet pour in some boiling water and BAM! Like a time-lapse on *Planet Earth* moving from winter into spring, you'll see the pot come to life. It's a miracle! It's also the closest most of us will get to eating space food, or the meals they eat in *Back To The Future 2*. If you're new to Pot Noodles, I suggest you start with Chicken & Mushroom. Bellissimo!

3) Peanut Butter

I've got no idea how it's made (I'm guessing it's got more than just the two ingredients), but peanut butter is truly a gift from the gods. Most people might settle for putting a little bit on toast in the morning, but for me the best use of the ol' PB is inside Arron Crascall's trademarked banana, honey, peanut butter and marshmallow fluff sandwich. It's so monstrous even Elvis Presley would have reservations about eating it.

4) Olives

Okay, if the adverts are to be believed, this one is genuinely good for you, actually. Although probably not in the quantities I eat them. This is what they call an acquired taste. I only got into olives because when I'd go out for dinner with Char, she'd order some when we sat down and as someone who can't ignore food, if it's in the same room as him, let alone right next to him, I'd always eat at least half whether I liked them or not. Now I'd say it's fair to say I'm addicted to them.

I remember the first time I tried a green juice. It didn't go down well. Literally. It was New Year, and Char and I decided to buy a NutriBullet. Everyone bangs on about them, so we thought what the hell, let's give it a go. We got all the stuff to go with it, and the next morning we treated ourselves to our first glass: banana, cucumber, celery, broccoli and you guessed it, kale. You know what, I hold my hands up here, it wasn't that bad. It was quite tasty, in fact. So half an hour later I loaded up the NutriBullet and had another one: more banana, more cucumber, more celery, more broccoli and yes, more kale. In just one of those glasses you can pack so much food. I don't think my body has ever had so many vitamins inside it at any one time. And again, fair play to them, I felt great. That day I left the house with a spring in my step and wandered into Morrisons looking for other interesting ingredients to try in tomorrow's juice. Ladies and gentlemen, I was now a juicer and I felt great. But not for long. Tragically, Arron Crascall never made it to the checkout that day.

I was coming up on the milk and cheese aisle when my body started to react. Within seconds, a sweat came over me, my guts started to rumble and out of my bum came the first warning shot – a gentle parp that was more than just a bit of gas. I panicked, threw my basket on the ground and sprinted for the bogs. All this Morrisons had was a disabled loo, and thank God it wasn't being used because the second my trousers got to my knees I just emptied all over that place. Seriously, we're talking a jet of green liquid shooting out for a minute straight.

When I was finally empty, I cleaned myself off and headed straight for the exit. Whatever was in that basket, I wasn't going to need it. The NutriBullet was getting packed away – which is where it remains to this day, gathering dust in the loft. Healthy people must be shitting all the time. Seriously, no wonder they're all so thin; down a green juice and you practically poop yourself inside out. Not for me, I'm afraid; I'd rather be overweight and in control of my bowel movements, thank you very much.

Back in the day (before the Green-Juice Age) food was proper – especially where I come from, as so many blokes had classic testosterone-fuelled jobs that involved chucking heavy stuff all over Dover's docks. They could not have done that on liquidised spinach, let me tell you – they left the house on a fry-up, had a proper lunch and finished with a sit-down meat-and-two-veg dinner. I grew up in a time when dinner meant sitting down at the table and having gravy with every meal. Mum would work her bum off all day and every night we all ate together. There were never any excuses; this was family time, and even if we were lucky enough to eat it on the sofas, the TV was off. Remember this was at a time when if someone told you you could pause live TV you would have called them a witch and burned them where they stood. Dinner time in those days meant missing out on some quality programmes, like *Neighbours*, *The Crystal Maze* or the ultimate heartbreak, if it was the weekend, *Gladiators*.

Sometimes I can't remember what I ate yesterday, but you never forget the food your mum cooks, right? My mum's special was chicken lattice pie, with the odd lasagne, chicken pasta bake or pot roast thrown in (not together, of course. Mind you, I wouldn't say no). Every meal had carbs – all the carbs, in fact – potato was king, and there was nothing sweet about it then, just good, honest stodge.

Now, this is controversial, but my kids are a bit of an

embarrassment on the food front – they eat dried apple, steamed salmon and rice cakes and my missus thinks this is okay. Sometimes I feel sorry for them as they will never know the joy of eight turkey drummers smothered in a tin of baked beans. Don't get me wrong, I can be good (like if I'm on a diet I will have the kebab and make sure I eat the salad and throw half the chips away), but where have all the turkey twizzlers gone? (Jamie Oliver, I'm looking at you). Are there really only salad bars in schools now? Surely the hot food and the iced buns were the only point of actually turning up?

Don't you think that nowadays everything feels like a trick? When you notice that pasta is actually 'spiralised courgette' (who honestly wants their Bolognese poured over chopped-up veg)? Salads now have things like charred broccoli and avocado shavings in them instead of croutons, caesar sauce or bacon. It's like when you were younger and your mum would hide the vegetables under the mash so you couldn't see them – you have to keep your wits about you and investigate a bit when you order nowadays – don't ever just assume.

Two reasons why I'm fat

1. I eat when I'm bored
2. I'm always bored

The one meal most at threat from this clean-eating revolution is breakfast. I firmly believe that the only problem people should face when it comes to breakfast is will I make the 10.30 breakfast cut-off at McDonald's? Take a look outside, though, and it seems instead the entire population are stressing out over whether the avocado they're ingesting is organic enough. Seriously, when did breakfast avocado become a thing? I honestly lie awake at night worrying about the future of jam, as everyone seems to prefer spreading 'smashed' avocado on their toast. What the hell does 'smashed' mean, anyway? The only thing that should be smashed at breakfast is the top of your boiled egg for a classic serving of dippy egg and soldiers.

Avocado to me will always just taste like green soap and lies. Seriously, how can you explain how the people that are obsessed with them have got rock-hard abs even though they're full of fat? 'Erm, it's because they're good fats,' they say. What the hell are 'good fats'? Fats are fats! These are the sort of people that like to say things that are so stupid they almost sound intelligent. The same people that in winter enjoy telling their friends: 'I reckon it's too cold to snow.'

Clean Eating also mean Raw Eating. Everything's raw. And really expensive. Why am I paying you a fortune for this if you're not even going to cook it? And it's not just in the fancy whole-food stores – take a look around on the bus and you'll likely find someone tucking into a supermarket bag of raw broccoli florettes like it was a bag of Pickled Onion Monster Munch. The king of raw food, though, is sushi, and I know it's nothing new but please understand, I had sushi for the first time only last year. And you know what? It's still a big mystery to me. Sushi is just raw fish and rice, so if you want that, just heat a bag of Uncle Ben's and pour it on a packet of smoked salmon. Et voila! You have sushi for about a tenth of the price. Also, pick up a fork and ignore the chopsticks. The first time I used them I had no idea that you had to break them apart, so I just plunged the joined sticks right into the top of a piece of sushi. At the time, I wasn't aware that you could actually bite into a piece, so I took one massive piece of sushi, covered it with red-hot wasabi and put the whole thing in my mouth. Obviously no one can have a clue what the sun tastes like. But on that day, in Yo Sushi at King's Cross station, what entered my mouth tasted like a solar flare had left our star, travelled one hundred and fifty million kilometres to earth, broken the planet's atmosphere, soared towards the surface and landed directly on my tongue. There simply isn't enough milk in existence to put out the fire that was in my mouth. So yeah, that sort of set the tone, really, for my non-love affair with cold fish and rice.

Clean eating is nothing new, of course. It's just a fancy modern way of dieting. I've had a crack at diets my whole life and they rarely work, they just make you unhappy. Well, you know what? I'd rather be a happy fat man than skinny and miserable. If you don't believe me, take a look at these genuine diets that are doing the rounds and tell me they don't sound like torture.

Genuine diets

The Atkins Diet

Yes, you know this one. You can only eat meat and veg, no carbs. Do you know what? At a push I might be able to stick to the Atkins. Don't get me wrong, I love carbs. (Oh God, I love carbs.) But it sounds like heaven to have the perfect excuse to go out for dinner and order a steak with a side order of steak. However, when you consider the main side effects are bad breath, constipation and icky farts, I'm 99 per cent sure that my family would leave me within a week. So sorry, it's a no from me.

The 5:2 Diet

Another popular one, this. For five days every week you can eat however much you want (Okay, I'm listening . . .) But for the remaining two days you have to totally starve yourself. I guess that sounds fair but I'm confident that if I was on it then two days a week hangry me will take over and I'll end up murdering someone. So I think it's better for society that I stick to The 7:0 Diet instead.

The Purple Diet

All you can eat are foods that are purple. That's aubergines, plums, grapes and I assume the purple ones in a tin of Quality Street. This sounds fun, but for some reason I've found it more difficult to eat aubergines since emojis came out.

The Paleo Diet

Apparently this is all about returning to our hunter-gatherer caveman roots, which means eating lots of seeds, nuts, fruit, veg and meat. I've not read into it too much but if this means having to physically stalk and hunt my dinner, then I'm afraid I'll be going hungry. Which I guess is the point of it.

The Hollywood Diet

For two days straight, all you can eat is this mysterious orange liquid which claims to have the right special blend of 'stuff' to make you lose ten pounds in no time at all. That sounds great. I've just got two very important points to raise. Number one: you do not eat a drink, you drink it – that's just stupid. Number two: the only mysterious orange liquid coming anywhere near my lips is Fanta.

The Maple Syrup Diet

This is supposedly Beyoncé's favourite: all your meals are replaced by a pint of water with a couple of spoons of maple syrup mixed in. Sounds awful, but I reckon I might have a better time if I combine The Maple Syrup Diet with my new Belgian Waffle Diet? Who knows, maybe by doing both these diets I'll end up losing twice as much weight.

The OMG Diet

The secret here is to skip breakfast and take cold baths. I assume it's named after what you shout the first time you get into that tub. If anyone dares suggest I skip breakfast, I don't care, OMG or no OMG, I'll be telling you to GTFO.

The Tapeworm Diet

Unbelievably there are people out there who deliberately infect their bodies with tapeworms in order to lose weight. The idea is that the little bugger lives in your intestines and consumes the food you eat so you don't have to. Sounds great, right? Except the fact that you have a bloody worm living inside you! And these aren't like normal worms you find in the dirt, either. These bastards grow as big as seventeen metres long. And what's more, at some point you're going to have to poo it out. Imagine curling out a seventeen-metre-long worm! 'Err . . . Are you okay in there, mate? You've been in the toilet for hours.'

Now, I'm not trying to mug off any fitness fanatics out there, but they think they're going to live longer than us by eating protein bars and protein shakes. Yes, that might be true, but I'd rather enjoy my food over my shorter lifetime than punish my tastebuds for the sake of a few extra years. Speaking of protein shakes, am I the only person who feels hungrier after drinking one? No amount of sludge can make my body stop expecting a breakfast that involves bread, brown sauce and meat. When I try and drink one it's like my body is saying, 'Yeah mate, I can see you're having a really funny day today. Nice one'. And don't get me started on how constipated they make me. Talk about a tough workout.

Of course, I've got nothing against people being healthy, that's all great, keep up the good work! I just think something needs to be done to take a bit of pressure off society and help the youth of today put down their Fitbits and CHILL OUT! Eat what you enjoy eating and have fun. Although take that with a pinch of salt (or not), as it's coming from a guy whose definition of clean eating is washing your hands after eating a pancake roll.

CHAPTER FIVE

TAKEAWAYS

Now you're talking! Who out there doesn't love a takeaway? No matter what's going on in your life, whether your choice is a Chinese, a curry, fish & chips or pizza, a takeaway is guaranteed to make your day. There's nothing better after a long day at work (in my case, running around town with my phone in the air asking strangers to dance with me), than getting that text from your other half saying, 'Fancy a curry tonight?' Oh, it's so good. In fact, I'm going to pick my phone up right now and text Char.

'How about I order a Chinese later?'

Sent.

Ask anyone their opinion on takeaway and they'll give you a detailed ranking of what they like. It's a deeply personal thing. Everyone has a favourite cuisine, and within that they have their go-to order. For me, my favourite is Chinese. Seriously, I love it so much that as soon as I was old enough to work I wasted no time getting a job in my local takeaway just to eat the free meal all staff got before their shift started. If you think I'm a big boy now, imagine how big I'd be if I still worked there! Hang on a second, Char's texted back:

'Are you kidding Arron? I've just been to the shops. Besides, we've had a Chinese three nights this week already.'

Ah. Okay. That's the thing about takeaways, whenever you're getting food delivered to your door, it has to be for a good reason. It can sometimes take a lot of convincing to justify ordering one, which is why it's always good to have some foolproof reasons to fall back on. These are a few of my personal suggestions.

Reasons for takeaway

You've been good all week!

Well done you. It hasn't been an easy few days. Especially as your office is in the middle of that Bake Off and Darren in Marketing brought in those salted caramel brownies. So treat yourself, and even if you end up undoing *all of* your hard work, remember it would have been much worse if you'd eaten Darren's brownies.

You've been bad all week!

You mean it this time – the diet starts on Monday.

You got a promotion at work!

Congratulations! Now with that extra bit of dosh you can treat yourself to *two* side orders.

You lost your job!

Time to drown your sorrows in a korma. Just don't forget to give your CV to the delivery man.

It's your birthday!

Traditionally, this is your classic excuse for going into the restaurant and sitting in instead. However, if you're keen to celebrate and would prefer not to put your trousers on (hey, it's your birthday!), then why not get a takeaway instead?

It's a Friday!

Always the perfect way to round off a week.

It's a Sunday!

You're back at work in the morning, so give yourself one last thing to look forward to before the rat race begins again.

It's a day!

Who are we kidding? You don't need an excuse. If you want to get a pizza, pick up the bloody phone and order one, mate!

Let's face it, the world is a bit glum at the moment, which is why I think now more than ever it's important for the nation to rediscover the joy of takeaways. I can't think of a great time in my life that didn't involve them. Okay, so I might not have taken my chow mein into the actual delivery room, but I definitely celebrated my kids' births with a cheeky Chinese. And I mean proper takeaways here, people, none of that Deliveroo bollocks. As I watch the poor buggers on their bikes loading up with £100 sushi and risottos for delivery, I shake my head. That's not a takeaway – that's basically having a posh dinner out, but on the sofa. I am talking about a curry where you always order two dishes more than you need and have the rest for breakfast; a pizza delivery with three more pizzas than you need because it's more cost-effective; a saveloy and chips with a cheeky gherkin; or a Big Mac meal and six chicken nuggets for afters, with two sweet and sour sauces in the Big Mac.

Speaking of McDonald's, have you been to one recently? They're amazing. They've basically managed to combine my two favourite high street chains: Maccy Ds and Argos. Seriously, you draw a number and wait for your Big Mac meal like you were waiting for a kid's bike and a new set of power tools.

That's the fun bit. Before that you have to shame yourself by typing your excessive order into a massive tombstone-like screen that pretty much broadcasts your order to everyone in the place. I'm actually all for self-service, but you might as well have a bloke with a megaphone next to you shouting your lunch order out, or one of them old-school town criers ringing his bell, all like, 'Hear ye! Hear ye! Arron has decided against the usual six nuggets on the side and ordered twenty-four instead! And who is he kidding, ordering a Happy Meal? He's clearly not got the kids with him. That'll be his starter, I assume! Mind you, the toy this week looks pretty sweet, so good job, Arron. We'll be seeing you again this evening, shall we?'

Takeaways are a lot of fun but they can often be the cause of some pretty bloody disputes. First off, there's deciding what to have in the first place. Me, I'd literally have anything, it's all great. But then there's those people (you know who you are) that say they like anything but then when it arrives they have an epic sulk because to them, 'I don't mind what we order' means 'If we don't end up getting fish and chips, I swear to God I'll punish you for the rest of the night with arm-folding, pouts and death stares.' But it's easy to go the other way; if everyone is 'free and breezy', you end up with all of you just staring at each other and nothing ever gets ordered. In this situation you need a decision-maker. A leader. If you ever find yourself stuck in this infinite state of purgatory, it's up to YOU to take action and decide. Everyone will thank you for it (except your mate 'sulky Carl', who even though he said 'anything is fine with me', actually only wanted Domino's).

Let's talk a bit about takeaway etiquette, starting with the oldest question in the book: to share, or not to share? Let me clear this one up quickly: Crascalls do not share. As soon as it enters the house, that tray is getting tipped onto my plate and no one else will get a look-in. I'm serious; I don't even share poppadums. And if anyone complains, the answer is simple: If you wanted Chicken Dansak, you probably should have ordered Chicken Dansak, shouldn't you? Mind you, your Butter Chicken looks nice . . .

Think I'm being mean? Well, listen to my next piece of takeaway wisdom: always tip the guy or girl that delivers your food, even if it's late or if you don't like their attitude. Whatever the situation, you can't ever forget that these people are in total control of your food between it leaving their kitchen and arriving at yours, so you might want to keep them onside. Upset them, and next time you order you can pretty much guarantee that *your* sweet and sour balls have been bunking up next to *theirs*, if you know what I mean.

Let me tell you about what takeaways really mean to me. They're more than just food; they're a family ritual. Every household should have a takeaway night – a special event that you all look forward to. In my parents' house it was always Wednesdays. Wednesday was payday for my dad, and he used to come home with a brown envelope of cash and we'd jump around excited because we knew that signalled Chinese. It's mad, really, but I can remember those envelopes so clearly and the feeling of pride I had for my dad and the excitement for what was coming every time he marched in holding them. I reckon my obsession with Chinese food could be almost entirely down to this routine. A psychiatrist would probably say that it's got nothing to do with the food at all, but what I'm actually experiencing is love for that moment, that closeness with my family and the joy that came from sharing it with the people that mattered most to me. And if that's really the case, then how can anyone argue that it's not good for you?

CHAPTER SIX

EXERCISE

You can't really talk about food without talking about exercise, can you? If you're a bit sick of this general area already then don't worry: based on the amount of exercise I do, you should be looking at a very short chapter. Everyone has a breaking point before saying enough is enough and they have to do something to get fit. For a lot of people this could be because they've eaten too much at Christmas, or because summer is coming up and they want to be 'beach ready', or maybe it's as simple as noticing that your jeans are starting to get a bit tight. For me, I know it's time for me to start exercising when I smile and I can see my cheeks without using a mirror.

Let me make one thing clear, mate. I have total respect for them, but for some reason, gyms and me just don't get on – I think that would be a fair assessment. For starters I look around most gyms and the machines look like they were designed to hurt me – all except the vending machine, of course, me and him have got a great relationship (I think I can do at least forty reps on that one). But as for all the other machines, I might as well be walking around an executioner's chamber, that's how brutal those things look. I'm not joking; I think I'd rather step onto a torture rack than anything you'd find in a Fitness First. Come to think of it, there's one machine I've seen that's supposed to help you with stretches that isn't far off being an actual rack.

And that's another one of the things right there. Why should you need a machine to help you stretch? All it is is touching your toes! I can do that at home, and I tell you what it wouldn't cost me – fifty quid a month. Of course that's not true. I can't touch my toes wherever I try it. The point is, though, if you want to exercise, you've got the whole world out there. You don't need to get to the gym every day to work out. To help prove my point, here's a list of things you can do at the gym that you can easily do somewhere else.

Exercises you can do at home

Treadmill

Okay, this is a no-brainer. It's just running! I don't care where you do it: outside, inside, in space; just run. And for the purists out there, if you want to recreate the full treadmill experience, put Sky Sports News onto an iPad and dangle that in front of your face at all times. Also, every now and then sprint flat out with the same utter terror as a person that's just accidentally set the machine to 20mph more than they can handle and can't find the off switch.

Free weights

Do you even lift, bruh? No? Well, you will with this cheat! All you need to do is find something around you to pick up and put down. It's that simple. Perhaps it's something you'd be lifting anyway, like a heavy book, a cup of tea or that box of *Friends* DVDs you promised Char you'd take to the charity shop but can't bring yourself to part with. In order to maximise your gains, make sure when you lift them that you hold your breath, scrunch up your face and over-exaggerate how much of a struggle it is to lift. Your face should be going bright red and your veins should begin to show. If you want to perfect this look, make sure you take a hand mirror with you to the toilet next time you're really constipated; your face does pretty much exactly the same thing whenever you're trying to squeeze out a rock-hard turd. After you've done a few reps comes the most important stage; rather than put the object calmly back down on the table or the floor you picked it up from like any normal human would do, instead just drop it from a big height and, as you do, remember to scream out loud a massive animal-like noise – the world needs to know you just lifted.

Bench press

This guys, is the most important weight routine. To perform a bench press at home, you're going to need to lie on the floor and lift something sturdy lengthways across your chest. For this, I find my kids are the perfect shape and at one, three and eight years old respectively, I've got a good choice of weights. If you don't have your own children, do you have any willing nephews or nieces? If not, I can't stress enough how inappropriate it is to try and bench-press a stranger's child.

Battle ropes

Battle ropes are all the rage these days. I don't know why; the last thing I'd want to take with me into any war is a piece of rope. At the gym, people just grab an oversized skipping rope and shake it until their arms get tired. I suggest you pop to your local toyshop and buy your own skipping rope or steal one from a child when they're not looking (just joking!).

Kettlebells

Recreate your own kettlebells at home by taking the kettle from your kitchen and putting a brass ball inside it. Now enjoy listening to it ring while you lift that kettle up and down. Okay, I'll be honest, I don't really know what a kettlebell is.

Lunges

This is just walking funny. You can do that anywhere.

Stretches

Stretches are really important. Don't undo all your hard work by failing to look after your muscles and getting yourself injured. There are little tricks you can do to help get a premium stretch from the comfort of your own home. For starters, put jam on your elbow and try and lick it off with your tongue. You won't get a better arm stretch in any gym. Next we need to stretch your legs. Have you ever tried missing out a step or two on your way upstairs? Well, this time we're going to be missing out six at a time. Yes, I know it sounds impossible and yes, it probably is incredibly dangerous but it will be worth it in the morning, I promise. Finally, get someone to rub a little bit of oil into the centre of your back so that a spot begins to form: a big, tender, juicy boil that's ready to go at any second. Now try and pop it. I promise you, by the time you eventually get your arms far enough round to reach it, you would have stretched out your chest, shoulders and back brilliantly.

The equipment in the gym is bad enough, but the classes are even worse. Have you ever tried spinning? If not, just imagine paying someone to pedal non-stop for an hour without leaving the same small windowless box. You're jammed so tightly against the people around you that you can lick the sweat off them like they were a Fab lolly (please don't actually try this. I'm pretty sure you can get into a lot of trouble. Especially if, like me, everyone else in the gym is significantly stronger and has a very high chance of beating you senseless). Spinning is basically prison. Albeit a prison with Fab lollies for cellmates. Here's an idea. Let's solve the world's energy crisis by hooking up every single spinning bike to a massive generator. Forget coal, forget nuclear, say goodbye to wind farms: we've just come up with the secret of green, renewable energy – fitness junkies.

Why are all gyms totally covered with mirrors? No one looks good when they're working out (except probably The Rock). If you ever caught a glimpse of me sweating in the gym you'd be on the phone to the zoo immediately, as you'd be convinced a bright red hippo had escaped its enclosure and was now tearing up the place in his finest activewear. We don't need to be staring at ourselves like everybody seems to insist on doing. I swear I look around and people are lifting up their phones for selfies more than they're lifting up weights.

Okay, let's talk about activewear, too, because is it just me or is everyone wearing their gym gear all the time at the moment? I understand people don't want to have to carry a change of clothes around with them, but do they wear it all day and then go to the gym, or do they go to the gym and then wear it all day afterwards? And who wants to wear their sweaty gym gear for any longer than they need to? Are you telling me all these people are comfortable sitting down to watch *EastEnders* wallowing in their own ball sweat? Mind you, since these Fitbits came around, every second is a workout for some people. 'Gotta get my steps in! Gotta get my steps in!' Okay, get your steps in, mate, but would you mind doing it wearing something other than a neon green wife-beater and a pair of shorts that leave nothing to the imagination?

Gyms try and hook you in by offering free trials. Well, let's try it the other way: I invite you lot to come and spend a day in my 'fitness centre' and see if it's the sort of lifestyle you can commit to. I promise you'll be hooked as it basically consists entirely of sitting on the sofa eating Celebrations in your pants while watching *Ex On The Beach*.

Have you guessed yet that I don't like exercise much? Well, that's not entirely true, though, as you see I love sport. Actually, that's not true either; I don't really like sport at all but to me, sport is an excellent excuse for going out and having a drink with your mates. And I love going out and having a drink with my mates. So by that logic, I could be one of the biggest sports fans in the country.

I can remember some incredible nights out that have all been directly linked to a sporting event. The Euros, the World Cup, the Ryder Cup, the Olympics, the Paralympics, The Ashes, the Lions, The Masters, Wimbledon. I've got no idea what actually happens at these events; I just remember having a great piss-up when they come around.

There's one night out in particular that springs to mind. It was after England got knocked out of The World Cup in 2010. I can't remember anything about the match (something about Frank Lampard scoring a goal but not really scoring a goal), but I do remember everything else. When the game finished, me and some mates had the same reaction as everyone else in the country – drowning our sorrows in a pint of beer (or ten). There was a lot of tension that night as everyone was pretty upset with the result, even though you'd think after all this time everyone would be pretty much used to losing. We'd done your typical tour of Dover's pubs, and it was on our way to our final spot that we landed ourselves in some serious trouble.

We were just walking along one of Dover's side streets – I wish I could say 'calmly', but who am I kidding, we were tanked up on beer and chanting football songs – when a car revved up from behind and mounted the kerb in front of us. This wasn't good. Did we offend someone earlier in the night? Did we spill a drink on someone's missus without realising? Did we somehow cross paths with the only group of Germans in Dover and piss them off with one of our 'patriotic' songs about world wars and world cups? Four seriously angry dudes got out of the car, but they didn't appear to be from Germany. They were Chinese. They walked menacingly towards us and I was shitting myself. I thought we'd somehow found ourselves in a gang war with the Triads (even though I'm pretty sure Dover isn't known for its Asian gangs).

As they marched towards us, it was clear they were only interested in me. 'Oh God, what have you done, Arron? What have you done!?' The guys were terrified, doing their best to fight them off as they grabbed hold of me and escorted me back to their car. But it was no use. In their drunken state my friends were helpless and just had to watch as they threw me into the back of the car and drove off. What did they do with me? What had I done to deserve being kidnapped by the Triads? Well I'll tell you. Firstly they weren't Triads. That was obvious when we got to our destination. They were in fact the waiting staff at a local Chinese restaurant. You see, a week before, I'd gone in, ordered a Chinese and left without paying – an accident, I assure you! It turns out that they were driving home from work when one of them recognised me, and all these blokes wanted was for me to pay the twenty quid or so I owed them and be on my way. So that was that; the debt was settled and half an hour later I was back home. But I waited until the morning before letting the guys know the truth. 'Kidnapped by Triads' sounds way cooler than 'forgot to pay for his sweet and sour chicken balls'.

So there you go. A memorable sporting moment that has nothing to do with sport and everything to do with getting drunk. With that in mind, the best sporting events are of course the ones that take place in different time zones, so you have the perfect excuse to be down the pub before McDonald's have even stopped serving breakfast.

Actually I take that back; the best events are when they're here in the UK. Surely the world must now recognise that we are better at hosting events than any other country on the planet. It's just like in real life – you've got some mates who are simply better at hosting parties than the rest. Like, the Rio Olympics was great and all, but compared to London it felt like something was missing. It had great atmosphere, it had great entertainment, it had great music, but still something wasn't quite right. It was like Rio was hosting a brilliant house party but awkwardly had forgotten to provide any dips. The whole world says what an amazing job they did, but deep down they're thinking, 'It wasn't quite as good as London. At least London remembered to buy salsa.'

Then you think back a bit further and you remember Euro '96. This for me was the pinnacle of sport in this country. Not even the Olympics tops it in my opinion, and as this is the single greatest sporting event I have ever witnessed (sorry, I wasn't around in '66), it's also the only one where I remember the actual matches.

England had some incredible games on their way through the tournament: smashing Scotland and Holland in the groups, and beating Spain in penalties in the quarter-final before having everyone's dreams crushed by losing to Germany through penalties in the semi-final (thanks to a pitiful penalty attempt from Gareth Southgate). The whole tournament was amazing, and it put the whole country in a frenzy all summer. Everyone was buzzing. In fact, it was the last time I think it was safe to hang an English flag out your window without people accusing you of being racist. We were Gazza-mad after Paul Gascoigne scored an absolute screamer against Scotland. The game was 1-0 late in the second half and Seaman had just saved a penalty to keep the lead for England. The Scots were rattled, and when the ball came over to Gazza he knocked it up in the air over a defender and – without the ball ever touching the ground – thumped it into the back of the net.

This is how important Euro '96 was. It made ME able to talk passionately about football! Although I should also point out that when Euro '96 was around, I wasn't old enough to drink so I wasn't down the pub on this occasion like I would be today. I'm 99 per cent sure that this is the actual reason why I can remember so much about it.

What was so special about Paul Gascoigne's goal is that just before the tournament he was ripped apart in the papers for getting smashed in a dentist's chair on a night out with the lads. (What bars have got dentist's chairs in them, by the way? Am I going to the wrong places? 'What will it be, Arron? The usual two Jäger Bombs and a root canal?') These days you hear all about the strict diets and regimes sportsmen have to stick to. Things they can and can't do. It's militant. I'd say they've got it tough, but come on, they earn an absolute fortune, right? I might be wrong, but even as someone who's not massively into his sport, I know that the England team have been pretty rotten for the last few years – they're always disappointing in tournaments and getting beaten by totally rubbish teams. Well, is it just a coincidence that this is all at the same time that they're forbidden from going out, having some fun and getting wasted on a dentist's chair? I tell you, if I ever became head of the FA, the first thing I would do is install a dentist's chair in every England training ground, and every one of them would be lined with shots for the players to down at their leisure. Do that, and I guarantee you they will win the World Cup . . . I think.

An emergency guide to talking about football

If, like me, football for you is more about sinking pints than scoring goals, you might feel pressure to contribute to a conversation you know nothing about. If that is the case, here's a rundown of some foolproof phrases you can say to hold your own and help ensure you won't be left out of the group.

'They're not using the channels enough.'

I have no idea what or where the channels are, but I heard some bloke say it once and everyone looked at him in total admiration. I've been using it ever since, and have enjoyed receiving the same impressed nods of agreement.

'What an incredible goal that was last night.'

Don't worry if you can't think of a goal. You have to realise there is *so much* football being played at any one time that there will always be an incredible goal last night. Maybe not in any of the English leagues, maybe not even in one of the European ones. If someone asks you for more details, just roll your eyes and walk away. They don't know about last night's goal? Then they're not worth talking to.

'He's not worth the money they pay him.'

No footballer is. Which makes this phrase, in football terms, an absolute tap-in.

'Your Rooneys, your Agüeros . . .'

For some reason, football fans love to talk about players in plurals; as if there was actually more than one Wayne

Rooney knocking about. Remember to bear this in mind when mentioning names. This is of course nonsense; if there were two Rooneys, then why would people pay so much for the one? It's basic supply and demand there, people.

'The refereeing has been shambolic.'

The great thing about the referee is that everyone hates him no matter what team they're cheering on. Yes, that makes him an easy target but you know what? When you're trying to bluff your way through 90 minutes of football (and the 15 minutes at half-time) you'll need all the easy targets you can get.

'I've heard Mourinho's got his eye on him.'

Maybe he has, maybe he hasn't but no matter what people tell you, no one really knows who Mourinho has his eye on other than Mourinho. This is a safe gambit. Unless of course you're talking about someone who already plays for Mourinho. If this happens to you, then now would be a good time to get another round in at the bar.

Homework

If you feel like you want to take your football bluffing up to the next level (perhaps there's a busy run of fixtures coming up, or you're going on a stag do this weekend), then you may wish to do some revision in your spare time. My advice on this occasion is to stick to the strikers. No one wants to hear what you have to say about (*googles Premier League defenders*) John Stones or Leighton Baines. Keep your focus strictly to the Rooneys and Agüeros of the world.

There was something else that was special about Euro '96. There was a song. But not just any old song. I'm talking about the greatest football terrace song there is, ever was and ever will be. I am of course talking about 'Three Lions' by Frank Skinner, David Baddiel and The Lightning Seeds. Play just the first couple of bars to anyone in England and you'll put a smile on their face as they remember that magnificent summer over two decades ago. This song defines England as a country; that's how important it is. It's running through our veins, it's in our bones, babies are born already knowing the words! I still don't entirely know who Jules Rimet is, but it doesn't stop me passionately belting out his name when it comes up in the chorus. Also, I am a massive fan of Baddiel and Skinner, but who isn't? In the summer of '96 they were as big a partnership as Shearer and Sheringham.

If I had my way, I'd find out what pub Frank and David were drinking in right now, I'd park outside in my car, wait for them to walk home then drive up behind them, mount the kerb and chuck them in the back seat. Then I'd drive the two of them and The Lightning Seeds (who I kidnapped earlier) to the nearest recording studio and force them to stay there until they wrote a new song. Something that can reunite the country again. Something to make people forget about political debates, forget about Brexit, forget that there's more to this world than hating one another. A new song from Baddiel and Skinner is exactly what this country needs right now. And if I need to get sent down for fifteen years for kidnapping to make that happen, then so be it.

CHAPTER SEVEN

TELLY ADDICT

It wasn't just their music that had a massive effect on me. Despite my limited interest in sport, Baddiel and Skinner's *Fantasy Football League* was one of many TV programmes that were important to me growing up. Remember this was before the internet, so our entertainment didn't come from Facebook or YouTube. If you wanted to watch something funny, you had to do more than get your phone out and flick through your socials. And I'm talking about before the days of Sky Plus or Netflix, too, so you couldn't just series-link a show or download it to watch on demand whenever you felt like it. Sitting down to watch one of your favourite programmes was an event; it couldn't be missed, and you couldn't afford to be the only one to go in to school the next day not having seen last night's episode of *The Fast Show*.

I've always been obsessed with comedy, and the '90s did comedy better than any other decade. You'll hear people bang on about Monty Python like it's the be-all and end-all but, while I absolutely love that lot (*Life of Brian* is one of my favourite-ever films), to me it doesn't come close to the likes of *Bottom*, *I'm Alan Partridge* or *Big Train*.

It's still crazy to me that there are people out there that have never seen *Big Train*. It's a sketch show that ran for two series in the 1990s and had the most incredible cast there has ever been: Mark Heap, Kevin Eldon, Julia Davis and Simon Pegg to name a few. Simon Pegg! People pay a fortune to go and watch his movies but I'm telling you, save your money and watch *Big Train* instead, mate. Pegg has been a massive influence on my videos, and all of his shows taught me loads about fast, fun comedy. (Simon, if you're reading, why not get a big fan like me a role in your next *Star Trek* movie? I reckon with a decent pair of sunnies and those massive Klingon ears I'd be able to perform some mad See Ya Laters.) *Big Train* was British comedy at its best. The sketches were short, silly and surreal and they didn't rely on swearing or doing anything offensive, which has always been something I've tried to replicate in my videos. One of my proudest moments over the past few years was when I was filming *Drunk History* and one of my comedy heroes, Stephen Mangan, came up to me and said how he liked my stuff, especially as he felt he could watch them with his kids knowing there wouldn't be anything dodgy in there. It made my day, but I'm pretty sure he was sick of me by the end of the job. Turns out he's pretty tired of people yelling Dan! Dan! Dan! Dan! at him all the time.

My favourite comedy of all time, though, is *Bottom*. I, like so many others, was brought up on *Bottom*. (Which is not a sentence I imagined I'd ever write.) It looks like the most depressing show you could possibly imagine. Two filthy blokes in an even filthier flat living out their filthy lives. Even the name of the show is filthy. Apparently Rik and Ade originally wanted to call it *Your Bottom*, so that people would go around saying, 'I saw *Your Bottom* on TV last night.' What more would you expect from those guys? Rik Mayall was a genius, and the world is a way less funny place without him around. Growing up, I used to dream I'd get a chance to meet him. Then, as my videos started to take off and opportunities came around, I began to see it as a very real possibility – I even dared to dream about possibly working with him in some way. And then sadly, out of the blue, he died. We've had a lot of famous people leave us over the last couple of years, but I swear that hit me harder than any celebrity death before or since.

But at least we still have all of his great work to remember him by. And if you haven't already seen *Bottom*, I suggest you sort yourself out immediately. Jump onto Netflix, Amazon, iTunes or whatever and find *Bottom* so you can understand its brilliance. In fact, while you're at it, you can make sure you tick off the rest of my comedy bucket list.

Arron's top ten TV comedies

1. Bottom
2. Only Fools & Horses
3. I'm Alan Partridge
4. Big Train
5. The Inbetweeners
6. The Office
7. Trigger Happy TV
8. Gavin & Stacey
9. Dad's Army
10. Spaced

In my day of course we didn't have On Demand of any sort; we didn't even have DVDs. Back then, if you wanted a constant supply of the shows you loved, you needed two things: a *TV Guide* and a long-play VHS tape. I was obsessed with backing up all my favourite TV shows onto a whole library of blank tapes. Whenever a programme was on that I loved, I would load up a VHS into the machine, wind the tape to the right point and hit record. Each tape could have up to six hours of your favourite shows – it could take months to fill one up, and believe me when I tell you, you don't know heartbreak like finding out that your dad had just taped over your *Red Dwarf* tape with six hours of snooker coverage.

The younger generation will also never know the hassle involved in having to rewind a tape. I can't believe I had the patience, especially when it came to finding a specific episode in a TV series. If you wanted to watch a quick blast of your favourite episode of *Friends*, it would take thirty minutes of rewinding and fast-forwarding just to find the specific one you wanted to watch. Or if you were lazy you'd just rewind to the beginning every time and watch the same first episode over and over again. The arrival of DVDs was a godsend. Honestly, if you're the same age as me you must remember the feeling of watching your first DVD. It felt like the future, right? For me, being able to jump to any episode you wanted at the touch of a button made it one of the greatest inventions of all time. They also brought with them another new phenomenon: the DVD menu. I would routinely fall asleep while watching a DVD and wake up the next morning to the menu on loop. Most of the time they were annoying as hell. The same ten seconds of music playing over and over again. However, fall asleep to the second series of *I'm Alan Partridge* and you were treated to something wonderful: an infinite loop of Alan in his motorhome playing air-bass to Gary Numan. If you've seen the show, you'll recognise the moment. I think it's amazing, but that could just be me getting brainwashed as it looped for five years straight while I slept.

You can't really talk about '90s comedy without mentioning a little TV show called *Friends*, can you? It's the only programme I can think of that is loved by everybody. Supposedly by the time it finished the main cast were paid a million dollars an episode each, which is a bargain if you ask me. I used to dream about living with Joey and Chandler – can you imagine what the three of us would get up to? I'd like to think it would be absolutely full of the best banter, but it's more likely I'd be stood in the corner with my jaw on the floor too nervous to even breathe because Rachel had just entered the room.

Do you ever wonder what that lot would be up to now if *Friends* was still going? I'd like to think that if it was, then these are some of the episodes they'd be making.

The One Where Ross Accidentally Sends a Dick-Pic to Monica
The One Where the WiFi Goes Down
The One Where Rachel Unfriends Monica
The One Where Chandler Wants to Netflix and Chill
The One Where Joey Goes on a Five-Day Juice Cleanse
The One Where Phoebe Forgets to Cancel During the 14-Day Free Trial
The One Where Monica Rents the Apartment on Airbnb
The One Where They All Play Minecraft *Instead*
The One Where Ross Was Totally Chirpsing Chandler's Mom
The One Where Ugly Naked Guy Has His Snapchat Hacked

TV has always been a massive part of my life, which is why last year, when BBC3 asked if I'd be interested in making a small sketch series I jumped at the chance. The idea was to pack each episode with a mixture of sketches, phone stuff with the public and mash-ups where I get cut into some massive movies and music videos. I'm really proud of what we created and had a huge amount of fun filming it, so you should hunt it down (your watchlist must be getting pretty big now).

The first recording day was a big one; off to the beach for a re-enactment of one of the most famous scenes in *Jaws*. It's the bit where Sheriff Brody (the copper in the film) first sees the shark. He's sitting there on the beach, and while everyone is larking about having a good time, he won't take his eyes off the water because he knows there's a shark knocking about. Sure enough, Jaws shows up and Brody yells at everyone to get the hell out of the sea. You'll probably remember it because there was this particularly great bit where the camera does this massive long zoom-in on his face. He's sitting there wide-eyed in shock (when really you know he's thinking 'I told you so.') It's a great scene, and perfect for us to take the mick out of in the show. The joke I had planned was to use all of Sheriff Brody's bits but when you see why he's yelling at people to get out of the water, you realise it's because he's spotted me and he's noticed I've just had a cheeky whizz in the ocean (come on mate, don't judge me. Are you telling me you've never let one go in the ocean before?).

Recording this sketch was going to be a fun start to the week except for one crucial thing: we were filming in October. I don't know if any of you have visited Deal beach in winter, but I'll tell you one thing, it sure as hell doesn't look like any beach I've seen in America. It was overcast, freezing, windy and had some of the biggest waves I've ever seen. Me and the director were rolling around in the water all afternoon and we didn't film a single second of anything useful. For starters you'll notice watching *Jaws* that the water is totally calm, so when we looked at the footage side by side it was pretty ridiculous how different they looked. Actually we should have included what we shot anyway. It was hilarious. At one point the director got hit by this one particularly massive wave, and because he was the one holding the camera you can see from the footage that he does about three or four backwards somersaults before crashing into the stony beach. And as for me, forget acting – I must have pissed myself at least twice out there.

This minor setback didn't stop us trying to get the shot, though, and near enough every other day the director had me strip off to my pants (in October, don't forget) and jump in the Channel. My bits retracted so much over those few weeks I think they went unseen until Christmas. Thanks, BBC!

Of course, working for such a respectful corporation as the Beeb meant that everything had to be done by the book. I couldn't just run around doing whatever, like I was used to doing. I remember one time we needed to get a couple of hits in Morrisons. Nothing major, just one or two See Ya Laters for the top of the show. Before we began I remember being sat in the director's car in the car park. He gave a pep talk about how we had to keep a low profile and not bother the staff or the customers any more than we needed to. 'Let's just walk in, get what we need and leave before anyone knows we've even been there.' I would do my usual work with the phone and as soon as we had a hit, he was lurking in an aisle nearby to get the punter to sign a release form to say they were happy to appear in the programme (like I said, everything had to be by the book). Half an hour in, we didn't have the footage we needed. I tried a few hits and I was getting rumbled before I got near, or the words I said came out wrong or the glasses didn't drop right. Things were getting tense; the director was worried that the staff were growing annoyed with us, so he took me into the wine and spirits aisle to give me another pep talk. He suggested that I back off for a bit; the staff were going to ask us to leave and now more than ever we needed to keep a really low profile. With that, he then took a step back right into a shelf of beer and sent crateloads of Desperado and Corona plummeting to the floor with a massive series of crashes. Then silence. We turned to each other and didn't know what the hell to do. So we just burst out laughing.

'Let's just come back tomorrow,' I said.

'Yes,' he replied. 'After you've done the *Jaws* bit in the water.'

When it comes to TV, I really feel sorry for the kids. They just don't seem to get the same joy as we did from running home from school to catch their favourite TV show. In my day the only thing that kept me going through primary school was knowing I'd come home to shows like *Byker Grove*, *Art Attack*, *Fun House* and my personal favourite, *ZZZap!* These days, however, whenever Alfie gets back from school all he wants to do is play on the iPad. *Minecraft* has a lot to answer for! Those kids' shows have had a massive effect on me: *Art Attack* taught me how to draw (and build a massive picture of a car out of duvets), *Fun House* taught me everything I needed to know about twins and go-karts and *Byker Grove* taught me to never ever go paintballing without adequate eye protection. You're never going to get that from *Minecraft*.

As a child in the '90s, the best TV was always on a Saturday. In one evening you had treats like *Blind Date*, *Noel's House Party*, *You Bet* and *Gladiators*. Everything these days is just singing and dance competitions. Back in the '90s all the entertainment you could ever want could be found in *Gladiators*: excitement, flair and some of the most impressive physical specimens you've ever seen squeezed into Lycra. For any of you that went through puberty at the same time as me, I'm pretty sure Jet must have been your first crush, too. Looking back I can see why Dad took such an interest in bonding with his son while *Gladiators* was on; at the time I just assumed it was the intense competition and athletic performances, but no; like every other bloke over thirteen he was probably tuning in just to see Jet wrap her impressive thighs around another victim, wishing it was them getting yanked off in Hang Tough. I meant yanked off the hoops, of course, not what you're thinking, filthbag.

And Saturday morning TV was even better. I remember setting

my alarm every week to get up early enough so I could watch *Live & Kicking* from start to finish. These days on a Saturday morning you've got cookery shows and news. That's like torture for any six-year-old, surely? *Live & Kicking* was such a big deal that even now I can still remember the phone number to call to enter their competitions. Seriously, now that everything's saved in my phone I couldn't even tell you my mum's number, and yet in an instant I can tell you what to dial: 081 811 8181. That's what you had to ring if you wanted to try and win a Game Boy with Super Mario Land and Tetris. Perhaps it helps that it had a catchy tune that accompanied it. ('Oh-eight-one, eight-one-one, eight-one, eight-one!') In fact, from now on I'm going to give all numbers their own little jingle to help me remember them. If you're thinking about trying it yourself, then I suggest you don't go singing your PIN number out loud when you're at a cash machine, otherwise you'll be in for a right Live and Kicking.

But growing up, not all TV was as good as I'm making out. Even now I'm haunted just by the sound of some programmes. For example, whenever I hear the theme tune to *This Morning*, or even the blast of 'duh-d-d-duh, d-duh!' they play in and out of the adverts, I'm hit by an overwhelming feeling of guilt. You see, when I was young, the only reason you'd be hearing that was if you were faking a sickie in order to bunk off school. (You know I'm right, did you try it too?) Back then, there was no shaking the horrible guilt I felt listening to Richard and Judy while resting my head on a radiator to convince Mum I still had a temperature.

Two other shows that have left a deep impression on me are *Songs of Praise* and *Antiques Roadshow*. When I was young, my nan loved these programmes and as I loved my nan, I was never going to deny her that fix of Christian sing-songs followed by an hour of looking at battered old gravy boats, but still to this day if I ever catch a glimpse of it, a wave of terror crashes over me like Deal beach in October. As these shows were on every Sunday evening, to me *Songs of Praise* and *Antiques Roadshow* will always be associated with the worrying feeling having to go to school in the morning. Even though I'm in my mid-thirties, as soon as I see or hear them, I suddenly start stressing that my geography homework is due in in the morning and I haven't even started it!

And while we're on the subject, someone sound the bell because it's time now to learn a thing or two about my special relationship with the wonderful world of school.

SCHOOL DAZE

Here's something you might not have been expecting: looking back, school was pretty fantastic for me, actually, you know? Sure, the classes were a bore and the teachers were tough – especially that headmaster, he was evil. But I studied hard, made good friends and got by with some great grades. Yes, it was awkward that every time I scratched an itch I transformed into a dog, but puberty's all about changes, right? Plus it didn't matter as long as I had my lucky 50p coin in my pocket; just give one side a rub and any wish could become mine. Not that I had time to play around with wishes – most of my free time was taken lining up alongside my school friends fighting intergalactic space monsters in our brightly coloured spandex, or conjuring a massive sodding dino-robot at will.

Okay, you got me, none of this is real. Well done for guessing, have a biscuit, mate. That was of course the combined plots of *The Demon Headmaster*, *Woof!*, *The Queen's Nose* and *Mighty Morphin Power Rangers*. All of which have left a stronger impression on me than school. And no, it wasn't fantastic for me; I wish I could sit here and tell you, 'School is great, work hard, they're the best years of your life!' But the truth is I hated every second of it, and there are very few positive things I can look back on. Well, there's one or two that would raise a chuckle, but for all the wrong reasons.

Let's start with primary school, and before we get into the nitty-gritty I think it's pretty important you get a solid idea of what young Crascall looked like, because I was exactly the sort of kid that if you spotted in the street now you'd go, 'Oh, I bet he has a tough time at school.' Yes I was overweight, but not in a funny, chubby kind of way, but more of a Channel 5 documentary kind of way. Seriously, flick to the picture section and take a look (like that wasn't the VERY FIRST thing you did after picking up this book!). It's hard not to look at pictures of young me and not instantly scream, 'Oh my God, that kid ate Arron Crascall!'

My primary years were spent at Shatterlocks Infant School in Dover, and later Barton Road Juniors. Looking back, my time there is a blur of polyester uniforms and sports days. It's hard to recollect specific details, but the one key thing I remember is a feeling of terror. For some reason I was scared of everyone and everything: my teachers, the other pupils, inside, outside, me if I got a glimpse in the mirror. I know it's a stressful time when you first start school, but this was years of walking about like a nervous wreck. What I wouldn't give to meet myself at that time and tell young Arron to man up. As scared as I was, you can imagine what assembly was like for me – being surrounded by hundreds of people in one location was pretty traumatic, like a scene from a zombie film, just with less brain-eating and more notices about after-school clubs.

To help us fill in the gaps, I've managed to dig out some school reports and original schoolwork from my mum's house, which will do a better job at describing how I was as a pupil. It all starts with a belter, and I'm not saying I was a star pupil or anything, but check out this poem I wrote when I was seven.

Arron Crascall, aged 7

Makes you think, doesn't it? It's got so much meaning to it. Yes, trees are important, but it's really all a metaphor for global warming and the complexities of the environment. It's a stark reminder of the delicate balance within our ecosystem, and how everything in this fragile planet is connected. Today the world is a divisive place; friends are turning on each other over polarising issues like immigration, equal rights and foreign policy, yet these two lines remind us of how we should put our differences aside for the greater good. Yes, trees make homes for squirrels, but you know what? Birds *also* live in trees, and until that clueless lot in Westminster realise that, the pretty world is in danger. So what do you think of that, huh? Not bad for a kid that still couldn't tell the time. And Ian, if you're reading and are still looking for a new tat to go alongside your misspelled 'See You Later', perhaps you could etch this poem into your other cheek?

For some reason, this genius wasn't appreciated while I was in primary school. It's clear when you take a look at excerpts from some of my school reports at Barton Road Juniors. Do you remember the dread of picking up your school report? Or the build-up towards parents' evening? Those were the worst, especially as I reckon I had the worst reports in my school. Why Mum has kept hold of them I have no idea; they weren't exactly the sort of trophies worth showing off to the neighbours when they popped round for a tea. Anyway, enjoy:

My primary school reports

His free writing lacks imagination + his spelling is weak. He does not write in sentences, but his handwriting has improved.

Lacks imagination? Did you not see the tree poem? I just created world peace with two sentences, love. Okay, yes, you've got me on the spelling; to this day my spelling is so bad even autocorrect has given up on me. Here's something I've learned about writing this book; there's someone who works at the publishers whose sole job it is to correct all my spelling mistakes. I think I owe whoever it is an apology. They probably have to work harder on one page of this than they do on the entirety of most books.

Arron still does not know his sounds as well as he ought, but he has made good progress. He does not have the ability to self-correct, showing that he is not understanding the text completely. He is able to learn pieces by heart + recite them clearly.

Does not know his sounds? What on earth does that mean? As in 'Arron doesn't know that a cow goes moo or a cat goes miaow or a horse goes quack?' I don't remember ever being *that* stupid. Hang on, I've just looked it up and realised horses do in fact go neigh. There you go, how's that for self-correction?

> Arron has not made as much progress as I would have liked, mainly because he is a poor listener. He can do so much better when he applies himself. He tackles practical work quite well but lacks understanding of basic number work.

All right, this one's not too good, is it? Lacking an understanding of basic number work is not the sort of thing you see on many Tinder profiles, right? Still, I'll take the compliment about practical work. Even if practical work in those days was just walking up and down the playground with one of those clicky wheels on a stick. If I went and did that now you're not exactly going to give me a PhD.

> Arron does not retain information very well. He is sometimes confused about what he is supposed to be doing in Science work & does not follow instructions.

Unless you plan on becoming a doctor or a physicist, science is pretty useless. Put it this way, when filming a video I've never had to know how photosynthesis works. And as for following instructions, I'm a man. Men don't *do* instructions.

> Enjoys drawing +has a good idea of shape. He is able to colour quite well.

I was ten when this was written. Ten years old and I'm getting praised on my colouring! And even then it's not amazing. 'Quite well'? What the hell does 'quite well' mean? 'Yes, Arron knew to colour the sun yellow but he couldn't keep inside the lines for shit.'

> Is generally well - co-ordinated He has a good eye for a ball+ can throw very well.

Again, ten years old here, people.

> Enjoys singing + is able to sing in tune. Does not mind singing alone!

I know exactly what you're picturing: a little Arron wearing his rubbish old Walkman headphones, shrieking out some Mariah in class just like in my awkward headphones sketches. Well, this was way cooler than that: boys and girls, I was in the school choir. Now remember, this is long before that Gareth Malone lad made choir-singing popular. In many ways you could say I was a trendsetter, ahead of my time. Barton Junior School was the scene of a revolution in high-pitched hymn practice. Well no, I didn't exactly pick up any chicks in the choir, but you know what, if the only thing I picked up from primary school was the ability to perform in front of strangers, then I'd say it was pretty important in the development of Arron Crascall, the bloke that sings in public for a living.

Let's move on to secondary school, which was a lot less fun. By the time I got to Astor College I was bigger, greasier and awkwarder. I had that special style of hair that was gelled forward into a line of shiny, rock-hard spikes. It didn't look that different to the spikes they put on top of fences to stop you climbing them. And probably would have been just as effective. I also wore the biggest hoop earring you've ever seen on a bloke that wasn't either Captain Jack Sparrow or a member of Right Said Fred.

The uniform at Astor included a white shirt with a black tie, black trousers, black shoes, black jumper and black blazer. If you're thinking to yourself that sounds a bit like an outfit for a funeral, then you're pretty much spot on. What still haunts me about the uniform, though, is rather than ordering it from the same place everyone else did, my mum insisted on cutting a couple of corners. For example, everyone in school had the exact same black pullover with this little school logo stitched into the fabric. Everyone except for me. My jumper was also black and also had the Astor logo, but because the fabric was ever so slightly different, and because the logo was a patch sewn on top rather than being part of the jumper, I was a target. What is it with kids that if someone is ever so slightly different, for whatever reason, everyone else turns on them like a pack of hungry wolves? Oh, and that's not all. My jumper had another special feature that no one else's had. My jumper had, wait for it . . . elbow patches. That's right. I looked more like a geography teacher than my own geography teacher! Mum says she put them on there to stop me wearing holes into the elbows, but considering the abuse I got for it, I reckon it must have been payback for some horrible thing I'd done to her. Maybe one day I forgot to compliment her on her chicken lattice pie. Can you think of anything worse than elbow patches? It makes you want to go back in time like the Terminator and put the young me out of his misery, doesn't it?

People at the school knew my mum well, thanks to an incident outside the school gates one afternoon that still haunts me to this day. When I was in Year 10, one of my classmates had picked a fight with a guy in the year above. I've forgotten what it was about, but like you'll probably remember from your school days, when there's a fight on the cards, you don't think about the details, you just want to see two people swing a couple of punches at each other before a teacher comes and calls it off. They were due to meet outside the gates after school and it was all anyone was talking about that day. It was going to be a massacre; what was my classmate doing, getting in the face of someone a whole year above? That's the school equivalent of a featherweight boxer going up a few divisions to face a heavyweight. The brawl went ahead, and as the competitors squared off against each other, a crowd began to form. What felt like half the entire school was now flocking towards this one small patch of grass around the corner from the perimeter fence. We all looked on; both lads were in each other's faces, each shifting their weight from left leg to right, anticipating the other's move, looking for an opportunity to try and counter the first punch. The crowd looked on. Hundreds of people silent in anticipation.

'ARRON! GET IN THE CAR PLEASE!' I knew who it was, instantly. The entire school took their eyes away from the action and slowly turned their heads in unison to see my mum standing beside the door of her luminous green Mini Metro. She was waving in my direction with a worried look on her face. Mum must have seen a fight forming and assumed her son had to be involved somehow. So there everyone stood in silence looking at Mum, looking at me, looking at the truly awful car. Then the laughter started. A massive stream of jokes and finger-pointing. I bolted as fast as I could towards Mum, keeping my head down to hide myself from the abuse: 'Oi, elbow patches! Mummy's here!'

I think the best way to describe Mum's car would be to tell you the nickname we all had for it in the family. Small, green and unappealing, it was 'the mushy pea'. If you think I'm overreacting, then either you've forgotten what it was like when you were young or you were one of the lucky people to get driven to school in a nice motor. The car you show up in at school is a very sensitive matter, and up until then I'd done a good job of keeping the mushy pea a secret, insisting she drop me off and collect me a good hundred metres away from another human in uniform.

On this occasion, the mushy pea, combined with her mumsy cooing, meant that if fighting someone in the year above was the manliest thing you could do at school, then I was currently at the complete opposite end of the scale. And if you want to know how the guy in my year got on with the fight, he lost. But it could have been worse; he could have been me.

It may come as no surprise to learn I was bullied at school, but you know what? I'm not going to give those bastards the satisfaction of even being mentioned in this book. That's one thing I learned when I started looking back on my school years, and it's something I wish I could have a chance to tell my younger self . . . All bullies are weak twats that are destined to live a life of loneliness and self-hatred. Today I've got a beautiful girlfriend, three beautiful kids, a beautiful home and a job I love. I'm even writing a book! What do bullies have? Loneliness and regret . . . Peace out. Mic drop.

The mysteries of school

There's a lot of odd things that I remember from school. Odd things that, if you talk to people, you realise every pupil has experienced and yet no one can explain. Here's a few of them.

Shatter-resistant rulers

People claimed that having a shatter-resistant ruler meant it would never break. If you brought one into school people would start queueing up like it was the sword in the stone, waiting for their turn to whack it against the table to try and get it to break – which of course it did. They all broke. We were fooled.

Nosebleeds

What is it about schools that causes nosebleeds? You rarely see adults spontaneously cup their noses to stop the stream of red pouring out of their face, but considering the amount of blood that could be shed on any single day, school would often look like a scene from a horror film.

The ink-eraser

Remember these? One half was pink, the other blue. The pink side was your typical pencil-eraser, but supposedly the blue side could rub out ink, which it did in a unique sort of way – it was so rough it rubbed a hole through the entire bloody page! What was the alternative, though? Tipp-Ex? That stuff was like plastering a wall. By the time you were done it was so thick you might as well be writing across a sludgy mountain range.

Gooood Moooorning Mr Craaaascaaaall

Why on earth is it that as soon as a group of kids try and say a few simple words in unison, it takes them FOREVER? I imagine it's so no one gets caught out calling their teacher Mum by mistake. Which of course was everyone's biggest fear throughout school.

School vouchers

We shopped for years at Tesco to get computer vouchers for school, and yet in all the time I was there I never saw so much as a new mouse mat. Did anyone?

Shedding your skin

Fooling your fellow pupils into thinking you were peeling off an entire layer of skin when in fact you'd just covered your hand in PVA glue. What a trick.

The test

Urban legend says that when asked in an exam to explain courage, one kid just wrote 'this' and walked out. They supposedly got an A. Which is total bollocks. Of course they didn't. This person's not real. And we were all stupid for ever believing it.

So school and me never really got on, and truth be told that was mainly because I just didn't want to learn. I couldn't find anything interesting. I'm not putting the blame on my teachers, but these days you see adverts about teaching where the kids are having a great time and the teachers are doing all these exciting tasks like building volcanoes and launching rockets into space. I hope there are schools out there like that because honestly mine couldn't have been further from it.

To be honest I've always had a bit of a problem with authority, which didn't work well for a hormonal kid in secondary school. I've had it my entire life and still do. Traffic wardens? Pathetic jobsworths without any sense of human empathy. Ticket inspectors? More of the same. Bouncers? Bullies with a badge and a bomber jacket. In fact, I'd say there's only two authority figures in the entire world that I respect and that's the police and the WWE boss, Vince McMahon. Seriously, he's, like, eighty, with arms bigger than my waist. Step out of line and he'd clothesline your head clean off.

Have you ever seen your teachers outside of school? My God is that weird, mate. It's like you've slipped into another dimension where someone normal is walking around wearing your teacher's face. A couple of months ago I saw one of my old teachers in a B&Q and to be honest it was really surreal. It was like meeting Lord Voldermort during his downtime. He Who Cannot Be Named needs help finding Rawlplugs: he promised Mrs V he'd build those shelves he's been putting off since Easter. When I met this particular teacher, he insisted I call him by his first name, which of course I couldn't bring myself to do. Have you ever tried it? It's weird to even accept they have first names at all, let alone say them out loud. No – I bottled it and called him sir instead. Sir??? I must have looked an idiot; I'm in my thirties!

Okay, I've told you what I think about my secondary school teachers; now I think it's time to share with you all what they thought of me. Yes, I've got another blast of school reports for you. Starting with my first year at Astor:

Secondary school reports

TEACHER'S COMMENTS:

Arron is a great character. He has really made progress recently, and is more confident about splatting tasks. A lovely nature and an ability to laugh at himself gives Arron a special place in the group.

How about that? A great character? A special place in the group? Maybe secondary school Arron wasn't such a dunce after all.

TEACHER'S COMMENT *Arron has a generally good attitude in English, and he is a good-humoured lad. He has produced some promising written work this year. Well done!*

I'll take good-humoured, definitely. And I even got a 'well done'. Seems like the teachers understood me more than I gave them credit for.

TEACHER'S COMMENT
Arron works well enough.

Okay, this bloke was clearly phoning it in.

SUBJECT *Maths*
NAME *Arren Crascall*   TUTOR GROUP *7DB*

SUBJECT TEACHER'S COMMENTS
Arren knows his tables to a reasonable standard and copes well with questions involving the basic four rules.

Of course, everyone knows the four rules of maths class are: 'Don't talk about maths class', 'Don't talk about maths class', 'Don't talk about maths class', and 'Don't forget if you hold the calculator upside down it spells BOOBIES.'

On to Year 8, and it's clear that this was a time when I was starting to explore my creative side.

SUBJECT..._Dance Drama_
NAME Arron Crascall   TUTOR GROUP 8DB.

SUBJECT TEACHER'S COMMENTS

Arron has his ups and downs. He started off with little self-control; then became more aware of his 'expectations' and produced a few promising pieces of work.

Yes I studied dance, get over it. Once you've let the image of a greased-up potato with a pirate earring pirouetting around a school hall fully sink in, can we discuss what she meant by saying my 'expectations'? Is she saying once I realised I was too fat to dance?

SUBJECT..._ART_
NAME ARRON CRASCALL   TUTOR GROUP 8 DB

SUBJECT TEACHER'S COMMENTS

Very Good Work

Another teacher who obviously had somewhere else to be the night they were writing reports.

SUBJECT..._Textiles_
NAME Arron Crascall   TUTOR GROUP 8DB

SUBJECT TEACHER'S COMMENTS

Arron has worked quite well in textiles. He passed his Sewing Machine Licence but he needs to take more care with his written work.

Yes, I own a Sewing Machine Licence. And you thought I couldn't get any cooler, right? Bear in mind also this is more than twenty years before I got my _driving_ licence, so I clearly had my priorities in check. Imagine trying to buy a four-pack of Smirnoff Ice when that's the only ID you've got in your wallet. 'Of course I can prove I'm eighteen. I assume a Sewing Machine Licence will do?'

On to Year 9, and the real Arron is starting to come to the fore; a kid who loved attention more than good grades. This is best demonstrated by the 'self-assessment' we all had to fill in at the end of the year. Please note, to help you further understand my abilities at school, I've left in all my original spelling mistakes (if only back then I had that publisher person to check over my work like I do on this book).

YEAR 9 PERSONAL STATEMENT

Name: Arron Crascall   Form: 9DB

I Like Astor scol because there is a lot of sense of humour the lessons are very good especklly art and Histo-ry Because I Like the teachers.

I think I had a better way with words with the tree poem at seven.

Next year I am going to try alot harder because I have been messing about to mush this year and I have got on report to much this year because I cannot concentrate in lessons because everyone talks to me

---

Firstly, I'm pretty sure I didn't mean I was 'messing about to mush'. That sounds painful. Secondly, look how I blame everything on the other people talking to me! There's no way it could have been me talking to them. I was the victim! I promise! Yeah, my teachers were having none of that. Can you see a pattern in some of the comments I received during my remaining years at Secondary school?

Year 9 Maths

When Arron can overcome the need to talk to classmates constantly he will be on his way to a higher grade.

Year 10 English

Arron should aim to concentrate all his efforts on his work in class, as he tends to be rather talkative.

Year 10 Science

Arron spends much of his time in class making an unnecessary noise.

Year 11 Design and Technology

Arron spends far too much time talking and not enough time working.

SUBJECT Science

NAME Arron Crascall   TUTOR GROUP 11AC

SUBJECT TEACHER'S COMMENTS

At times, Arron has shown he has the potential to achieve in this subject. Unfortunately he prefers to gain attention from his friends by being the 'class-clown' which is distracting and time wasting.

It wasn't just a problem with me talking all the time either. My attendance was terrible. I was so uninterested in my classes that I would turn up in the morning, go to my lessons and then after lunch I wouldn't go to a single class (I warned you, guys, I'm not a good role model for how to get the most out of school). I would leave with my friend Stuart and head back to his house, which was always totally empty. His brother had a set of decks and we'd spend our afternoons in his room mixing drum & bass and jungle music. I got pretty good at it, which should come as no surprise considering half my time at school was spent there spinning tracks by Micky Finn, Kenny Ken, DJ Fenn and Shy FX. I always knew I couldn't make it with Maths or English or Science or anything like that. Those afternoons were probably the time I realised I was destined to entertain for a living. All right, these days I'm not exactly a resident DJ at Pacha lining up drops to thousands of sweaty twenty-somethings chewing their faces off in Ibiza, but if you've seen any of the videos of me dancing to drum & bass classics outside St Pancras train station, you'll realise I'm not that far off it.

If I had one regret about my time at school it's that I didn't pay more attention during History. These days I absolutely love history. Maybe it's because I'm getting older and more reflective; maybe it's because I just play a lot of *Call of Duty* (proper *Call of Duty*, none of that robot suit bollocks) but the real reason, I think, is growing up in Dover. If you're looking for history, come to Dover; it's absolutely full of it.

It all starts with Dover Castle, which is absolutely massive. You can see it from anywhere in town, and even now that it's coming up to a thousand years old it's still in incredible nick. It's always been the first line of defence from people invading from Europe, and it's never been defeated. That's worth showing an interest in, surely? Aside from its use in all the wars, for a long time it was a sort of holiday home for England's kings and queens. Again, how many people's little towns can boast that? 'Oh, you see that house on the top of the hill there? That's where the King pops over for a cheeky Easter break.'

Then if you walk around Dover, everywhere you look there are loads of other, smaller castles, little forts here and there and tons of cannons jutting out of cliff faces. The days of us getting attacked by a bunch of foreigners bowling up in a longboat are gone, but you can imagine at the time, if you were one of the French hoping to start some trouble, Dover must have felt like the final level in a video game, it's that fierce-looking. Even with infinite respawns, you and the rest would have struggled to make it any further than the Londis on Market Square.

By the way, how am I doing at describing this? Do you feel engaged? Because you know what, I'd love to do a history documentary one day. Imagine my teachers' faces if they saw me walking round places explaining stuff, playing the role of teacher myself. I reckon I could be all right at it too. I'd even dig out my old school jumper with the elbow patches for that classic teacher look.

If you're reading this and you're currently going to school, I know I say that I'm a bad role model and everything, but there is something you can take away from my experience. I hope you can look at me and realise that all that school stuff is not as serious as everyone makes out. There's more to life than learning about coastal erosion or long division or Charles Dickens. I mean, look at me, I was terrible at school and now I'm making a living uploading stupid videos.

And I'm not the only one. I've been doing a bit of research and it turns out Alan Sugar off *The Apprentice* left school with just one O-level and he's now worth over a billion pounds! By the way, an O-level is what old people call GCSEs. Then there's Simon Cowell, he left school with only two O-levels, got a job delivering letters around a record label and now he's one of the most famous people in the world. Finally, you should learn a thing or two about Richard Branson. He dropped out of school at sixteen without a single qualification at all and look at him now – he's worth almost four billion pounds and in the process of building a bloody spaceship! Ricky B's all, like, 'Exams? Nah mate, I'm going to space. SEE YA LATER!'

CHAPTER **NINE**

LOVE

What genius thought it would be a good idea for human beings to go to school, study, learn and sit important exams that decide the rest of their lives, at the same time the species goes through puberty? Were they insane?? These are probably the most important years of our lives, and while all that's going on, the only thing we can think about is the fact that Stacey in 8G smiled when we made eye contact during Chemistry.

I've got to tell you, if I had my way our school system wouldn't properly begin until puberty was well and truly over. You can go through Infants and Juniors just like normal, you know, learn the basics: reading, writing, that urinals are only meant for weeing in and not for you to sit inside and squeeze out a tiny turd – like I said, the important stuff. However, after you leave Juniors, all kids should leave school, to do what exactly I don't know – maybe hard labour in the mines or up chimneys (look, if I had all the answers I'd be knocking on Number 10 right now demanding an audience with the Prime Minister). The point is, absolutely no further education until the boy or girl reaches eighteen. I swear, that way every teacher will have the undivided attention of their students. Sorry Stacey in 8G, the only chemical attraction I'm interested in today is the bond between sodium and chlorine to form the ionic

---

compound sodium chloride. You see? This is my point! I'm thirty-four years old and had absolutely no problem looking that up on BBC Bitesize. I mean, sure, I still don't understand a word of it, but twenty years ago I wouldn't have even got that far. I would have opened my laptop and spent the rest of the night on MSN Messenger talking to my mates about how in school that day you could just about make out Stacey in 8G's bra strap.

Has love always been this difficult to manage? It seemed like a simpler time for Mum and Dad's generation. They met in the Townsend Club – a snooker hall right in the heart of Dover. There was a little disco inside twice a week, and like any of today's clubs (no matter how rubbish they are), anyone who was single would flock to it, looking for a bit of a flirt and boogie with the opposite sex. The women would dance in a circle around their handbags while the men looked on from the bar deciding which lucky girl was going to get a chance to go home with them. It was like an old-fashioned cattle market. (By the way, Mum, if you're reading this, I'm in no way trying to imply you do or ever did bear any resemblance to a cow, it's just a metaphor. Be kind to your mothers, people). These days all the power is with the girl. Us blokes are pushed to breaking point with the lengths we have to go to to impress the opposite sex, but back then, under the disco lights of the Townsend Club in Dover, all a man had to do was pick his moment and strike (by the way, Mum, if you're still reading this, I'm in no way trying to imply you are or ever were easy – once again, always respect your mothers, guys). Back in 1970 the Townsend Club was a goldmine for horny young men. But when you consider that in the very next room there was a depressing collection of frayed snooker tables and dodgy old geezers with pork scratchings in their beards and fags on their breath, there was very little competition out there for the likes of Papa Crascall.

This will likely come as a complete surprise to you, but in my late teens I was in full swing and actually pretty good at wooing ladies just enough for them to look past the extra chins, the spiked fringe and that hooped pirate earring. By this time I had learned that all it took was a good sense of humour and a lot of confidence. It also took a lot of planning and in my heyday, it required getting the boys round for some serious planning. Like we were trying to pull off a heist. Think *Ocean's Eleven* but instead of Hollywood heart-throbs like George Clooney and Brad Pitt sat around casino blueprints, it's a group of greasy teenage boys in Ben Sherman shirts and Kickers huddled round an N64.

Every one of our plans centred around the same location: Toppos. Toppos was the pinnacle of fine dining in Dover. Step through its swanky doors and no matter how bleak your relationship situation was, you'd come away more loved-up than a couple of newlyweds. Forgot your anniversary? Get yourself to Toppos, mate. Said another woman's name in your sleep? Toppos. Your wife surprised you at work and caught you doing the nasty in the stationery cupboard with Sue from Accounts? Table for two, please!

Whenever a girl went on a date with young Crascall, she knew she was in for a good night. They would be treated to whatever their hearts desired. Money really was no object, and that's because all of my dates were paid for by Mum. Looking back, I still don't know why. Perhaps she's just a hopeless romantic, but more likely she knew I needed a serious wad of cash to make up for my various flaws. Getting the money off her, though, meant running the gauntlet: telling her the girl's entire backstory, hearing her run down the usual dating advice (don't let her pay for anything, don't forget to compliment her, don't do all the talking) and letting Mum critique my outfit; doing a twirl as she says, 'Go on, let's have a look at you then.' Back then my standard date night ensemble is what I would call 'The *American Pie* look': Adidas Campus trainers, khaki trousers and a freshly ironed Ben Sherman (thanks for that, too, Mum). I would have perfectly gelled hair and even went through a phase of wearing beads, as I thought it made me look sophisticated, well travelled and in touch with my emotions.

I'd always treat my dates to a cab ride to the venue, but in order to make Mum's money stretch as far as possible I'd make sure I'd walk to just around the corner from her front door before ordering it. And the treats didn't end there, oh no – I was the ultimate gentleman back then. We would get there and it would be all opening doors for her and 'after you' as I pulled out her chair. Thanks to Mum and a very thrifty taxi ride I could confidently pass her the menu and say, 'Choose whatever you want', and it was often here that the next step of the heist – sorry, the date – would take place. We would be casually looking through the menu when suddenly there'd be a bang on the window and we'd look up to see my mates standing there behaving like idiots.

The first few minutes after you've just sat down is officially the most awkward part of any date. Making small talk can be excruciating, and is often the difference between third base at the end of the night or a polite hug and a goodbye. Me and the boys had worked out that the perfect way to overcome this was for the remaining guys not on the date to walk past and do awful things like wrap their arms around themselves pretending to be mid-snog or shout through the window something romantic like, 'Get in there, my son!' My mate Nick would even perform the ultimate act of sophistication and lift his shirt and push his gut against the glass. I'd fake embarrassment and come in with my killer line:

'Sorry about them, they are just my boys. I told them I was going to be here with a beautiful girl. I was so excited and they didn't believe that I would be out with someone so hot, so they've come to check you out. Hope you don't mind?'

She would giggle and blush and be all like 'shut up', as she hooked her hair behind her ear and looked down at the table. What a flirt. Another slam dunk, boys, well done. Because Toppos was right next door to The Firkin; one of *the* go-to pubs for young people on a Friday night, this sort of operation was never a bother for the guys outside. Everyone would be on their way down there anyway. You get in a rhythm when you're young, don't you? From the moment you find a pub that you manage to get served in at sixteen, you don't ever think of going anywhere else.

One good thing about being just outside the best pub in Dover meant there was never any doubt where each date would move on to next. And if for whatever reason the date was a disaster (we've all had them ones, haven't we?), you could always sack it off and rescue the night sinking pints with your mates afterwards. If anyone walked in after a bad date, we'd all chip in for a beer so long as they told the others every grisly detail of how horrible it was.

'Yeah, it was going really well, then we got to talking about her family and I accidentally-on-purpose told her her mum was really hot and the whole thing never really recovered. It was meant to be a compliment, for God's sake!'

The only problem with this was Dover is so sodding small that if the date *was* a disaster, then chances were she'd escape to the Firkin too and be at the other end of the bar telling the exact same story to her mates.

Yes, not every date went off like clockwork. One of my worst was pretty much not even a date. I remember one girl I really liked wouldn't go anywhere without her entourage of mates. Mama Crascall was generous, but there was no way she was going to pay for me to take nine girls to Toppos. Instead I took her on a good old-fashioned trip to the cinema (standard, right?). Sure enough, the entourage came too and now I was faced with a whole new challenge: getting to sit next to the right girl. From the second we met up I made sure not to leave her side. As we lined up for our tickets, queued up for popcorn and to get our tickets stamped I was stuck to her like glue – It would be worth putting up with this unnecessary rabble of screeching girls so long as I got two hours of uninterrupted one-on-one time next to her once the film started. Or so I thought. At the very last minute my bladder failed me and I had to go and have a piss. Did she wait for me? No, of course not! Did she save a seat for me inside? Did she fuck. When I returned, the lot of them had taken up an entire row and I was left having to sit behind her, on my own, stuffing my face with popcorn and occasionally smelling her hair.

Terrible chat-up lines

In order to survive out there in the dating wild, I had just two tools: my confidence and my humour, and back then there was no better way to showcase both talents than a good chat-up line. Here's a little rundown of my old favourites.

Are you a parking ticket? Because you've got fine written all over you.

Well, here I am! What are your other two wishes?

I'm sorry, but you owe me a drink. [Why?] Because when I saw you across the room I dropped mine.

Is your name Wally? Because I feel like I've been searching for you my whole life.

No? Well, then is your name Jacob? Because you're a cracker.

No again? Okay then, is your name Ariel? Because I really think we mermaid for each other.

Do you sleep on your stomach? If not, then can I?

Can I follow you home? Because my mum and dad taught me to follow my dreams.

Come to think of it, I'm not surprised that last one never worked, it's a little bit stalker-y, isn't it? Promise me you won't try that on.

I always wonder if it would be a lot easier playing the dating game today. It certainly *looks* a lot simpler. I've never used Tinder, but by the looks of things all you need to do is spend five minutes on the bog swiping right and you end up with a list of girls ready and waiting. But then again, I don't know if teenage Arron would have taken a good display pic (just take another look at the photo section if you need a reminder). If Tinder was around when I was that age, my picture would have been swiped left so many times it would have got whiplash. You know it's true.

Also in my day there was no smartphones. So when you went on a date you had each other's total undivided attention. It also meant you needed good chat if you were to survive and, as every single one of my teachers would agree, I was not short of conversation at that age. These days if you're out on a date you won't leave the house without setting up a Whatsapp group to give your mates a play-by-play commentary of how things are going. That sounds good, but it's not that great if you're the one left talking to yourself while the girl on the other side of the table is more focused on her phone, letting all her friends know how the idiot across from her just spilt Bolognese all over his shirt.

Thanks to technology there's no such thing as a blind date now, either. These days no one meets anyone new without giving them a good snoop on Facebook first. I feel sorry for all the girls who were sold a blind date with me: 'Yeah, he's bulky – in a good way. Jolly-looking, you could say?' If we'd had Facebook back then it would have been one quick search and bang, suddenly she's remembered she has a totally not-made-up wedding to go to that night. I've got a theory about Facebook, that because we spend all of our time looking at people we've never met, when you meet someone in public and they go, 'You look familiar', you can 100 per cent guarantee that it's because your face popped up during one of those marathon scrolling sessions through the 'people you may know' section. Not that you can trust anything you see online. You don't have to be a genius to use a flattering filter. I actually make a pretty damn cute rabbit on Snapchat.

Also, once you've had a thorough stalk of someone on Facebook, what's left for you to talk about on the actual date? You already know how old she is, where she lives, her place of birth, where she went to school, the names of her friends, her family, her pets, what she did on New Year's Eve, where she went on her holidays three years ago. The only question left to ask is, 'Who's that bloke with his arm around you in the photo at Becky's pool party in 2001?'

These days it seems like taking your relationship to the next level is made easier, thanks to social media. If my single mates go on a good date, all they need to do is send them a friend request on Facebook and hope they accept it. Then if things get really good they might even send an 'in a relationship' request. It's all very low-risk. Back in my day, however, you had to walk the green mile to them in the playground, entering the lions' den surrounded by all her mates, then with one deep breath ask: 'So, you seeing other people? No? Yeah, me neither. So shall we just see each other? Cool, see ya later.'

If I had the same technology then as I do now, I'd still provide the lucky lady I'm dating with a taxi ride to Toppos, but I'd make sure to treat her to a Mercedes Uber. If that wouldn't guarantee me third base, I don't know what else would. Having said that, back then my fingers were so fat I'd probably end up ordering an Uber Pool Prius by mistake.

One good thing about dating in the '90s was that without Google Maps, instant access to the internet and constant messaging on your phone, you had to work a lot harder to make plans. If you were going on a date then everything had to be set in stone in advance; you couldn't just wing it on the day. Also, you wouldn't want to change plans. To do that meant calling her up on the landline, which was horrific for two reasons. First of all, nothing was private. If your family weren't gathered around you listening to your call you could bet they were listening in on the second phone in Mum and Dad's room. Secondly, you had to deal with the gatekeeper on the other end. You'd pray she'd be the one to pick up, but more often than not it was her mum – or even worse, her dad.

ME: 'Hello sir, is Hannah around please?'
awkward silence
HIM: 'Who wants to know?'
ME: 'Arron Crascall, sir . . . We're erm, err . . . I'm her friend from college.'
HIM: 'That so? Never heard of you.'
more silence
ME: 'Well, you see, we're in the same—'
HIM: 'Hannah! There's someone called Darren on the phone for you!'
MUM (LISTENING IN): 'Going well, honey!'

Impressing a girl on a date was all well and good, but the true test came when I had to bring her back home. Whenever I went out to meet a girl, the family would spend the entire evening in the front room waiting for me to get back. No matter what time it was, they were expecting a full debrief, and if I came back with the girl she would have to endure the most intense welcoming committee you can imagine. There was no avoiding them, either; the front door to Mum and Dad's house opened up straight into the living room. There was no sneaking in – oh no – you opened the door, walked in and there, literally right in front of you, was my family, staring at you like you were the latest box set on Netflix or something.

Dad would be there, alongside Mum, my sister Amy and Auntie Cagol. (Don't worry, mate, it's not her real name – as a kid I could never say Carol so said Cagol instead and it's one of those things that's just stuck.) If there was a girl with me, Amy would be giving her the evils. As protective as a Rottweiler, she was. Mum would just smile and go on about how pretty she was, and within a minute Dad would be on to the story of how when I was born they thought I was a girl and were going to call me Zoe. He'd laugh his head off while whoever I was with would laugh along politely, making a mental note to call me Zoe for the rest of her life.

We would leg it straight up to my room, door firmly shut and lie on my bed as there wasn't room for any other furniture (at least that's what I told the girls). Just as we were getting comfy, me being all smooth and trying to have a bit of a kiss, we would hear this voice booming up the stairs. That would be my nan, who was always far less approving of bringing girls home than the rest of my family.

'Don't you dare bring shame to this house, boy!'

Nothing kills the mood quicker than being made aware that on the floor beneath you there's a seventy-year-old woman judging you.

Once me and a girl had a few dates under our belts, and Toppos was in danger of becoming a bit stale, I'd often treat a girl to a romantic meal chez Crascall. This would often mean walking back to mine via the local Chinese, sharing a pancake roll for the final leg of the walk home. I'd always call ahead, and Mum was so keen to help me make a good impression that when we got in and went straight up to my room we'd find two plates with knives and forks laid out right there on the bedroom floor. Classy, right? While it may be very difficult to imagine now, back then the sexual tension was massive. There was no denying it; at some point the romance would hit boiling point, those prawn crackers would be chucked aside and we'd start going at it. It was only a matter of time before that lucky lady was going to get the snog of her life with me running my sweet-and-sour-covered greasy fingers through her hair. Nothing says romance quite like Chicken Chop Suey.

Arron's Snog Mix

While digging out various bits and bobs for this book – school reports, photos and that – I stumbled across something pretty special and I think now is the right time to share it. Did any of you reading this used to make mix tapes when you were young? It's a lost art – the closest thing to it these days is making a playlist on Spotify. When we were young, to record a mix tape took some real graft: you had to line up the cassette to exactly the right spot, then hit play on the CD you wanted to record from while simultaneously hitting play and record together on the tape deck you were recording to. It was a system designed exclusively for people with at least three hands. It took so much determination that you could give it to someone as a gift and it showed how much you cared. My best creation by far was *Arron's Snog Mix*.

My Snog Mix was a 90-minute rollercoaster of romantic tunes guaranteed to make women melt in your arms. If I put this on when a girl was round, I'd be surprised if we weren't snogging each other's faces off by the time I had to flip it over to Side B. Now if you want a slice of that power, I suggest you grab yourself a two-deck sound system, a ten-pack of TDKs and get to work creating this masterpiece:

SNOG MIX – SIDE A

1. 'Dance With My Father' – Luther Vandross
2. 'Penny Lover' – Lionel Richie
3. 'If You Were Here Tonight' – Alexander O'Neal
4. 'Stay' – Lisa Loeb
5. 'Erase/Rewind' – The Cardigans
6. 'Half the World Away' – Oasis
7. 'Truly Madly Deeply' – Savage Garden
8. 'If You're Not the One' – Daniel Bedingfield
9. 'She's Like the Wind' – Patrick Swayze
10. 'Holding Back the Years' – Simply Red

SNOG MIX – SIDE B

1. 'Don't Dream It's Over' – Crowded House
2. 'Wicked Game' – Chris Isaak
3. 'With or Without You' – U2
4. 'If You Ever' – East 17 (Featuring Gabrielle)
5. 'I Want to Know What Love Is' – Foreigner
6. 'I Swear' – All-4-One
7. 'I Believe I Can Fly' – R. Kelly
8. 'Save The Best For Last' – Vanessa Williams
9. 'Is This Love' – Whitesnake
10. 'Don't Let Go' – En Vogue

Okay, I know what you're thinking: 'Arron, I very much doubt that a man with your self-confessed awkwardness and, err ... unique appearance would be banging women left right and centre as you appear to be implying.' Well, let me tell you, you severely doubt the power of a good sense of humour and a lot of confidence (not to mention a killer snog mix tape). My family was just as surprised as you, so much in fact that my dad once told me to stop treating his house like a knocking shop. One day he even arranged for his mate John to sit me down to have a special talk with me. If you thought having 'the talk' with your parents was bad, imagine having it with one of their friends. I only remember two things about my special talk with John. One was the casual 'Hey buddy!' approach he took, which included leaning back on his chair with his hands behind his head like he was the coolest supply teacher in the world. The second was a piece of advice that still to this day confuses me. He said that the moment you have sex for the first time, your ears pop. You know, like when you're going up in a lift too fast or through a tunnel (make your own jokes there, guys). Of course that makes absolutely no sense, but it still doesn't stop him, every time we meet, giving me two thumbs up and yelling, 'Hey, Arron! You lost your ear wax yet!?'

Also, yes, you're absolutely right, mate. For most of my teenage years it was incredibly difficult for me to get girls to even notice me, let alone sleep with me. When I first started to be attracted to girls I was a total mess, but all good things come to those who wait, and my God, I waited. Okay, get ready to take pity, it's time for you to hear about the many difficult years.

CHAPTER TEN

GET REAL, ARRON

For me, the long wait for acceptance by the fine girls of Dover began all the way back in junior school, where I was obsessed with one girl in particular. For the benefit of the tape, let's call her J. J was the prettiest girl in school and it wouldn't have taken a genius to guess that this particular obsession would only end in heartache for me; I was very clearly punching well above my weight, and considering the size of me at the time, that would have been some challenge.

I was nine and she was in the year above me, which meant our lunchtimes were spent in separate playgrounds. It was a forbidden love, you could say, like Romeo and Juliet. And just like them there were walls between us. I'm not kidding; the closest I could get to her was spying at her through the playground fence, watching her while she ran around with her friends. Wow, okay, reading that back it doesn't sound as romantic as I thought. Yeah, I was pretty much a stalker. But like all stalkers will tell you, my heart was in the right place. For almost a year that's how I would spend my lunchtimes until the worst happened: we all got a year older and J moved up to secondary school. It was the first of many times that this body of mine would take a heavy punch to the heart.

Going for girls that are well out of my league is a trend that has stuck with me my whole life. For all the years I was looking for love, I always fancied the prettiest girl in the room even though it was highly unlikely she even knew I existed. Before I hit my stride, if I told a girl how I felt, the chance was pretty high that she'd just look at me, tilt her head and go, 'Ahh, bless you.' Those three words haunted me for years. Even to this day I'm still punching above my weight. If you ever met Char, you'd realise she's way too good for me, but lucky for my kids I must have weak genes because they look more like their beautiful mum than they look like me.

Okay, let's move on to when my struggle got real. It was when I moved to secondary school and my hormones were in full swing. All I could think about was getting a girl to say three words to me that weren't 'Ahhh bless you'. Believe it or not, it actually didn't take that long, as within a couple of years I had almost every girl in my year talking to me. The problem was, the conversations were all the same: it was hot girls moaning to me about their boyfriends. I had found myself well and truly in the friend zone, people, which is an almost impossible place to claw out from. Every week I'd have a different girl on my shoulder crying about whatever shocking thing their fella had done that morning. Most of the time it was probably something utterly stupid like forgetting their six-week anniversary or sitting next to a different girl in Physics. 'Go out with me!!' I'd be screaming inside my head. 'I'd sit next to you in Physics! I'd sit next to you in Maths, too! And French! And English! And History! Wherever you go I'd sit next to you!' Yeah, school was a difficult time when my left shoulder was the only part of me coming close to getting some action.

I remember a school disco in Year 9 was my first proper attempt to break out of the friend zone. It was a familiar scene; just by turning the lights down and throwing in a smoke machine the school gym turned instantly from 'PE kit lost and found' to 'Ministry of Sound' – or at least, that's what it felt like to the hundreds of kids desperate to impress with their Adidas popper trousers (don't get popped!) and cheap aftershave they'd nicked from their dads. Can you remember your school discos? Maybe I'm on my own here, but why when I picture it does it seem nothing like they do on TV? In American movies they're these massive events that genuinely look better than most clubs I've ever been to. None of them have the rows of tables lined with paper tablecloths and orange squash that they had at my school discos.

Whether or not your school disco looked more like the epic prom nights you see in America or the lame three-year-old birthday party vibe ours had going on, there's one thing all school discos in this country have in common: the girl/boy split. You know what I'm talking about – all the girls lined up on one side and all the boys on the other. It was like we were lining up for an epic medieval battle like in *Braveheart* or *Game of Thrones*. The forces of the men lined up across the climbing wall, while the army of women lined up beside the crash mats. And in between us, the squeaky, laminated gym floor was our no man's land. If I was there now I'd finish off the *Braveheart* analogy by painting my face white and blue and riding up and down the line on a horse giving the other lads a pep talk before battle commenced.

Sons of Astor College, I am Arron Crascall.
I see a whole year group of my fellow men standing here looking to score with at least one lucky girl tonight. All you want could be a dance, or a snog, or perhaps you want more. Men, you could go out there now, try and impress them and end up dying on your arse. Or you could leave now, safe, with your dignity intact. But the months and the years will pass and at some point you will end up dying on your arse, I assure you. So wouldn't you trade all the days from this day to that for one chance, just one chance to

*come back here and tell our enemies that they may take
our dignity, but please, I'm begging you, please will you
take . . . OUR VIRGINITY!!!*

That would never work, of course. I wouldn't get the horse through
the door.

In my day, if a boy did pluck up the courage to cross no man's
land, it would feel like the longest walk of their lives. Everyone
would be watching, pointing, waiting for the drama to unfold.
And this boy wouldn't be going all that way to ask a girl to dance
with him. No, he'd be on a diplomatic trip to parlay on behalf of
another boy. Peace-talks would go along the lines of this:

BOY: 'My mate Dean really fancies you.'

GIRL: 'Which one's Dean?'

BOY: 'The one doing skids under the basketball net.'

GIRL: 'Yeah, all right.'

The school disco I want to talk about took place in Year 9. It was
like any other; jumping around to House of Pain or 'Boom Shake
the Room', confident that my chances of dancing with any of the
girls were non-existent, until I noticed a girl in the corner of the
room crying. By this point I had enough experience to know that
all crying girls were pretty much my responsibility, so I went over
to offer my shoulder.

'Just rest your head in the dent left by all the other girls,' I might
as well have said. The girl was L, and it turns out L's boyfriend was
kicking off outside and making a scene as he was being refused
entry. He was older, and more importantly went to a totally different school, so why he was so shocked that he was being bounced
was anyone's guess. Me and L sat there, in the corner of the gym
out of sight from everyone else. I listened for ages as she moaned
on and on about the chump outside; how she warned him not to
come and how he'd embarrassed her, and why does she have to be

with someone so hot-headed? Why couldn't she be with someone nicer?

That was my moment to strike. All the pieces were in place: I was nice. I was really nice. If all she was after was nice then I was the man for her. I had even scrubbed up for the night: I had a brand new shirt, blue with white collar and cuffs, freshly ironed, too (thanks Mum), and of course my trademark hooped pirate earring and well-greased spider fringe. But most importantly of all, I had a girl beside me who just might have been desperate enough to agree to a dance with me. This was it.

'Do you want to dance?' I mumbled. She slowly looked up towards me, her face red and blotchy from the tears, and nodded.

'Sure,' she said.

GET IN!!!!

I took L's hand in mine and proudly led her to the middle of the dance floor. People were looking on. 'Oh my God, is she going to dance with *Arron*?', 'Is Arron going to score?'

'Let them look,' I thought. I wanted the whole school to watch. Perhaps now they would learn that the days of treating Arron Crascall like nothing but a piece of meat to cry on were over. We found a spot just as 'Truly Madly Deeply' by Savage Garden came on – which could be the most romantic song in the world, ever – her arm came up to my neck and I reached around her waist, bringing her gently towards me. L fitted perfectly against me, her head resting on my chest. We were a perfect couple enjoying a perfect moment to a perfect song, and everyone was there to witness it.

One slight problem, though. She cried throughout the *entire* dance. I mean, proper sobbing. Like to anyone who didn't know the full backstory, it was like I'd grabbed this poor young lady and was forcing her to rock back and forth in my arms against her will. And everyone was there to see it. I had a lot of teenage girls crying on me in my teenage years, but that one was the absolute worst.

Savage Garden finished and we let go of each other. L patted me on the arm, wiped her nose and left the venue to join her boyfriend, leaving me alone with nothing but a memory, a glass of weak squash and a trail of snot right across my smart blue shirt.

Arron's pin-ups

Like every teenage boy, I made up for the lack of real women in my life by covering my bedroom walls with famous women who were just as likely to have sex with me as any of the girls from school. Here's my top five.

1. Saffron from Republica
2. Gwen Stefani
3. Britney Spears
4. Pamela Anderson
5. Gemma Atkinson (Bit awkward – Gemma and me now have the same manager so we bump into each other a lot. Although absolutely not in the way I dreamed of doing as a kid.)

Honourable Mention: Sian Lloyd. As far as I know, there were never any posters of her available at Woolworths, which is a shame because my room would have been full of them. I always had a special place in my heart for this weather girl. Sian, if you're out there reading this, call me!

Despite the great steps I made that night getting L to dance with me, it would be a good four years before I actually got someone to agree to go out with me. I was at college by this point, and not much had changed – I was still a big boy, I still had the exact same terrible hairstyle and the same terrible taste in earrings. I also still had the same terrible attitude towards education, only now, instead of nipping off at lunch to DJ at Stuart's, me and my mates would disappear to a pub for the afternoon. We were only seventeen at the time, but I don't think the staff at any of the pubs in Dover minded; after all, we gave them a lot of business. We'd even spot the odd teacher in there with us. You'd make eyecontact with them and there'd be this unspoken arrangement – 'You don't tell anyone you saw me here and I won't tell anyone I saw you, capiche?'

I remember one random afternoon I was at the bar buying a pint (giving it the biggun when what I really wanted to do was buy an Archers and lemonade) and there, across the room, by the jukebox, I saw my next crush: E. I was hypnotised. She had cropped dark hair, with striking lipstick and leather trousers; in fact, she was a near carbon copy of a certain lead singer from Republica. To this day I still remember the song she put on – it was 'Live Forever' by Oasis, which was ironic because tragically she died the very next day. THAT'S A JOKE! Sorry, a terrible joke, I couldn't help myself with that one. Jesus, I'm going to burn for that. But yes, she really was playing 'Live Forever', which will always be one of my favourite songs of all time.

Like all of my crushes she was well out of my league. Not least because she was in the year above me. And every time we'd accidentally make eye contact, E would make me go weak at the knees. She would smoke roll-ups and drink double vodka and Coke AT LUNCHTIME, which at the time was incredibly sexy. These days it's more difficult to pull off weekday, midday spirit-pounding – I remember a girl catching my eye last year as she slammed back double vodkas over lunch in a Wetherspoons in London, but there was something about the way this lass puked into her ham, egg and chips that somehow didn't have the same charm.

When she wasn't in class, E would spend her time drinking at Fleur's to more Oasis, and cruising around Dover in her mate's Metro to the Stereophonics. I, meanwhile, spent my days watching her from my usual position, of far away, making do with the times we'd make eye contact and she'd give me a pitying smile – which of course my mates teased me for. So far, so normal. I was on track to follow my usual cycle of crushing disappointment. Until Paris.

Paris was one of those typical school trips. You know the scene; a busload of overly excited teenagers off their tits with the excitement of not having to be in class. Across the Channel, we went round the usual sights: Eiffel Tower? Check. Arc de Triumph? Check. Notre-Dame? Check. But nobody would take anything in; we were all more interested in showing off than showing an interest in Paris. Every now and then someone would go for a wander and return to the rest of the group with a new thing they'd bought in a back-alley shop that was guaranteed to impress: weird foreign chewing gum, bangers and the Holy Grail of any school trip – porno cards.

E was on this tour, and she was all I could think about; after all, we were alone in the city of love. Okay, we weren't alone, we had about thirty schoolkids there with us, but I only had eyes for her, so we might as well have been alone. E also only had eyes for one on that trip – a particularly hunky litre bottle of Malibu she had tucked into her bag (what a woman). Part way through the day she'd run dry, which was bad news for her and great news for me. I suddenly had a purpose. A reason to exist to her. I did the most chivalrous thing I could do – run out and buy her some more Malibu.

Let me tell you, mate, if you're an underage kid struggling to persuade off-licences you're old enough to buy booze, I'll give you a bit of advice: go to France. They don't give a damn how old you are! I walked in, and could have come away with whatever I wanted, despite my boyish looks. Although on this occasion, I couldn't walk away with anything I wanted because I didn't have any bloody money left (damn you, porno cards!). This was my big opportunity to prove to the girl I had an unnatural obsession with that I was more than just the guy awkwardly staring from the bar at Fleur's; I was a man who could love her, protect her and provide for her (well, provide Jamaican coconut-based spirits for her). Lucky for me, the geezer behind the counter clearly took pity on me, and accepted my measly two francs for a miniature-sized bottle of some French Malibu knock-off. Okay, it wasn't ideal but at least it was something. We were due to meet at the bus any minute to make our way back to dull Dover which I luckily made at a sprint (well, I wasn't exactly weighed down by the bottle).

I got to the bus too late to sit anywhere near her, so I waited until we were on the ferry to make my final approach. Like a prowling lion stalking a herd of gazelle, I waited until E had separated from her friends before making my move. She was on the top deck, alone, lit up perfectly by the low setting sun. I knew this was my best shot so I walked towards her and held out my prize. Seeing the bottle there, dwarfed inside my fat hand, I suddenly realised how pathetic it looked. And how pathetic I must have looked. Oh God, this was a huge mistake. What an idiot, Arron.

But she laughed. She thought it was hilarious, in fact; to her, only an idiot would have bought a bottle this small on purpose, so it had to have been a joke.

'Arron, you're hilarious!' she screamed, and she grabbed me by the collar and brought me in for a kiss. It was a perfect scene; the sun was disappearing behind the horizon and France's coast was fading into the distance. If it wasn't for the few dozen pensioners sat at their benches, rolling their eyes at us and tutting in disgust, it would have been a perfectly romantic scene. Oh, and not to

Here you can see two interesting things about my mum and dad: 1) how much taller my mum is and 2) WHY IS MY DAD WEARING MY FACE??? My parents are so ahead of the curve – this is decades before Face Swap was even a thing.

Even the eldest child can suffer from hand-me-down hell.

My first birthday! Remember I told you my mum spoiled me? They clearly spent so much on presents that they couldn't afford carpets and just had to use leaves from the garden instead.

My first day of school! It's not my <u>complete</u> uniform though. I still had to put on my sleeves and, of course, my PLEASE BULLY THIS KID sandwich board.

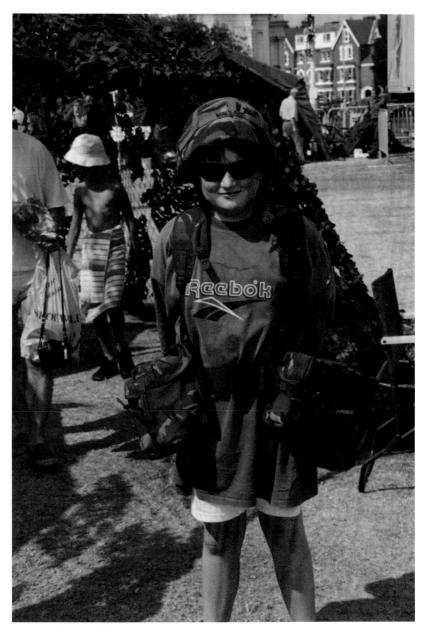

I'm not sure why this one's in here to be honest. All I can see is a random kid in a towel.

Carnival with the lads. This is what happens when, in the 90s, your two main style influences are Keith from The Prodigy and the Go Compare man. If you can't tell, I'm the big yellow guy on the left.

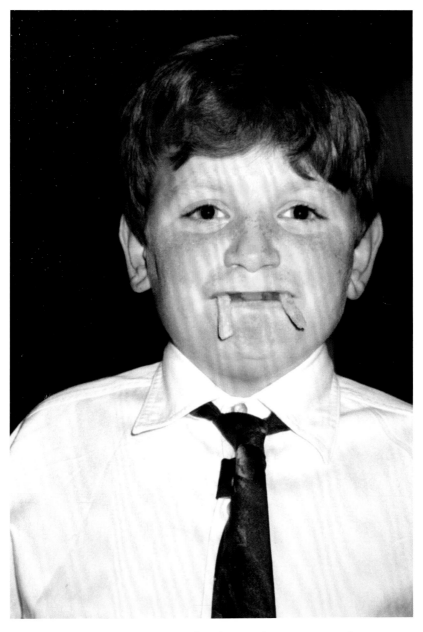

If you're reading this book looking for advice on how to get into the prankster game, you can't go wrong with the old fangs made out of salt 'n' vinegar chipsticks routine.

This is me, Amy and my dear Nanna. Nanna's the one in the chair by the way.

Hands down the most special day of my life. The moment I became a father for the first time.

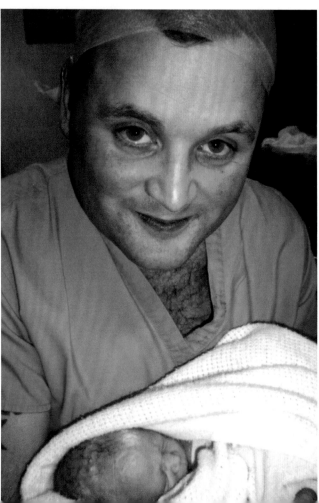

This is me and Char celebrating Will and Kate's wedding. I know what you're thinking: 'What on earth does a girl like that see in him?' I don't know mate, I ask myself that every day.

If you're reading this poem thinking 'ah, that's sweet' then do what I should have done years ago and look up what it's used for before running to your local tattoo parlour!

How can you expect anyone to concentrate when there are Babybels in the house?! This book probably would have been twice as long if Char had bought Dairylea instead.

mention my mates lining up against the window humping the air. Not exactly the 'king of the world' scene from *Titanic,*

But I didn't care. This kiss, my friend, had marked my transformation from Arron the awkward guy looking on from across the room to Arron Crascall, superstud.

CHAPTER ELEVEN

LOSING IT

Paris was amazing. Thanks to that miniature bottle of Malibu, I now had more spring in my step than a fresh pair of Air Max 90s. But I still didn't have a girlfriend. E went back to spending her days with her friends and I went back to staring at her from the other side of the pub. Thanks to that kiss, however, I had more confidence, and knew deep down that it was only a matter of time before she would be my girlfriend. I actually started to enjoy the chase; we'd still catch each other's gaze like before, only this time instead of looks of pity, she'd smile and wink. It was exhilarating. For the first time in my life I was being flirted with. She made me feel incredible; until one night I was looking at her across the pub and she wasn't looking back any more. No, she was snogging someone else, right there in front of me. You idiot, Arron! Two weeks ago you were staring at an open goal and now you've lost it all. So much for the thrill of the chase.

That night I left the pub to drown my sorrows someplace else. Somewhere private, in dignity, where E couldn't see how hurt I was. I didn't get far, though, settling for the pavement just over the road. I must have been making a bit of a scene, too, because it wasn't long before E came running out to see how I was. (So much for feeling sorry for myself with dignity.) This was my moment, and there, underneath the glow of the lights of Pizza Pronto, I finally said what was on my mind. I took a step towards her and poured my heart out:

'What happened in Paris was incredible. The best day of my life. But you mean so much more to me than just a cheeky school trip kiss. Whenever we're in the same room, my stomach ties itself into knots. And whenever we're not, all I can think about is you. I can't imagine a world in which I can't call you my girlfriend because you mean the absolute world to me, and yes, I'm not the best-looking guy out there, and no, I'm not the cleverest either, but I am honest. So you can believe me when I tell you there's no other man alive that will work harder to make you happy every single day, and if you give me a chance, I promise I will spend the rest of my life making sure you never regret it.'

Unfortunately, due to overwhelming nerves, those words didn't quite come out as intended. I managed to bark them all out in the space of half a second in one huge, deafening bark:

'WHARGHPT!!!' The noise was so loud, E backed away from me and lost her footing on the kerb. She went flying backwards into the road, and with her went my chances of having sex before I was thirty.

I was stunned. I didn't know what the hell to do, and while any normal human being would have rushed to her aid, I just stood there and watched in total disbelief. Well done, Arron, you've made a fine mess of that one. After what seemed like forever, E eventually sat up, adjusted her hair and laughed. What is it with this girl that every time I cock up, she just laughs? I've got to say, mate, if you're ever feeling a bit drunk there can't be many experiences in this world more sobering than accidentally frightening a girl you fancy into a heap on the road. As E sat there laughing, I bent down beside her and offered my hand. I lifted her to her feet and totally went for broke:

'Will you be my girlfriend?' I asked.

'Sure,' she replied, awkwardly hopping on one leg.

'Shall we get a pizza then? I'm starving,' I said, holding open the door of Pizza Pronto for my first-ever girlfriend.

Seventeen years old, and I finally had a girlfriend! But what the hell was I supposed to do with one? I didn't have a clue. Obviously I knew the important stuff – Dad's mate John had seen to that – but if I was ever going to get a girl to make my ears pop, I needed to know what the day-to-day rules were. I swear if women could just give us a set of instructions to follow that would make life a lot easier. Back then I had so many questions. Like how often was I supposed to call her? Did having a girlfriend mean I could never talk to another girl again? Was I supposed to play it cool if other blokes flirted with her?

But the main question was – how long were you supposed to wait before you slept with your new girlfriend? Lucky for me I didn't have to wait for long.

We'd been officially girlfriend and boyfriend for five months, and after spending all that time in the same few pubs around Dover, she invited me to a night out in one of the clubs in her hometown of Folkestone. My mum, who was as desperate as I was to transform me from awkward teen into local Lothario, drove me there. We were travelling in the mushy pea, of course, but fortunately she agreed to park it in a side street well away from the view of anyone so as not to blow my chances before the night had even begun. Mum even bought my ticket home, she got me a seat aboard the last train home, giving me as much time as possible to seduce my new girlfriend.

I met E at her choice of venue; a hideous place called The Harp, which was my first and only experience of a goth bar. I'm all for people expressing themselves with how they dress (come on, I wrote a whole chapter on skinny jeans) but it doesn't change one simple fact: Goths. Are. Terrifying. I'm not talking about your entry-level dressed in black, heavy on the eyeliner goths, I'm talking about spikes every-bloody-where goths. Spikes on their shoulders, spikes on their boots, spikes through their ears, through their noses, through their tongues and I'm sure through a lot of other things kept out of sight. It was like an AGM for The Road Warriors Appreciation Society.

Lucky for me I wasn't intimidated for long, spotting E across the sea of spikes. Dressed head-to-toe in black, she fitted in a lot better than me in my blue and beige *American Pie* outfit (Mind you, at least the pint of snakebite in my hand was black.) The heavy metal they were playing was a deafening mess of scratchy guitars and high-pitched screams. I leaned right into E's face every time she wanted to speak, all the while regretting that pre-match packet of Roast Beef Monster Munch I had seen off to line my stomach before I left the house.

'What time's your train!?' she shouted.

'Monster Munch!' I replied. She looked confused and asked again:

'What time are you getting the train back!?' I leaned in closer to answer:

'Roast Beef! Sorry, I thought I had some gum in my back pocket but it was just a receipt I left in the wash!'

She shook her head and reached into my pocket. She pulled out my wallet, ripping apart the Velcro and finding my ticket inside. She held it up to my face and tore it to shreds, throwing the pieces in the air like confetti.

'You're staying with me!' she shouted.

Jesus. Christ. I was intimidated before, but now I was totally shit-scared. Did that mean sex? Oh God, it meant sex. I made an excuse as quickly as possible and bolted for the toilets. I stood there, shaking, frantically texting every single one of my mates.

Three texts later I was done, staring at the mirror, getting my game face on and dabbing the sweat from my armpits with a pile of hand towels. The texts were rolling in. The usual lot you'd expect from a bunch of teenagers:

'Get in there, son!', 'Sorry, who is this? I don't have your number.'

I texted my mate Scott asking for a few pointers (and a lift home in the morning!). He said I should try picturing my mum having sex in order to try and make it last as long as possible. Which as gross as it sounds made sense, I guess.

The rest of the evening was a constant battle to not go and fuck it up. As the snakebites kept coming, I got increasingly drunk, and increasingly worried I was going to say something to ruin what was pretty much a done deal. I remained in this state of high alert, concentrating hard on everything I said and did. I remember at one point she asked if I was okay as I hadn't blinked for half an hour.

After The Harp we headed back to hers, tiptoeing around so as not to wake her parents. We crept into her room and the rest, I'm sorry to say, is a total mystery to me.

Throughout the entire time I lost my virginity, all I could think about was what I was going to tell my friends the next day. Scott, Hunter, Bear, I hope this doesn't freak you out, but I was thinking about you the whole time. In fact, not the whole time there were ten key stages of thought:

1) This is amazing! Can't wait to tell the boys about this!
2) What was it Scott said? Oh yes, picture Mum having sex.
3) Ew, gross.
4) Seriously, this is horrible.
5) Wait, does this mean Scott also pictures my mum having sex when he's having sex?
6) Oh God, now I'm picturing Scott and Mum having sex together!

7) WHY AM I THINKING THESE THINGS!?
8) MAKE THEM STOP! PLEASE MAKE THEM STOP!
9) Wait, why is she staring at me like that? How long has it been since I last blinked?
10) Have we finished already?

Does it even count as your first time if you weren't concentrating through it? When Scott arrived the next morning to collect me in his Nova he was full of questions, none of which I could respond to with a good enough answer. You want to know how it was? Well just picture me banging your mum for five minutes and tell me how enjoyable that feels!

E and I continued to go out for a while. I'll always be grateful to her for being the first person to give the chubby chancer that I was, a go. However, I wasn't grateful for the time she dumped me so she could get back with her ex. What can I say? It was the '90s and he had a soft-top Escort RS. There was no way I could compete with that. It would still be at least another fifteen years before I could even drive, let alone own a car. The only secret weapon I had was my Snog Mix and there frankly weren't enough sides on that to stand a chance with Mr White Escort. In the aftermath of the break-up, I might as well have changed the name of those mix tapes to my Broken Heart Mix because it took a long time to get over her. Mainly because I had to watch her getting dropped off every day in the car with her new (old) boyfriend.

Here's some advice for any budding teenagers looking to make it in the world of relationships. What I would give to be able to travel back in time and pass this information on to my younger self.

1) No girl out there is too good for you.
2) Be careful of the friend zone. I'm not saying don't be there to

offer women a shoulder to cry on, but make sure you don't end up being looked at as 'just one of the girls'.

3) Never stop making mix tapes (or playlists, I guess).

4) Having a car trumps everything. You could be a total prick with a face to match and still the girls will come flocking. So make sure you pass your test early and save for some wheels!

5) When you do finally come to lose your virginity, concentrate on the moment and cherish it. Don't spend the time picturing your best mate knocking boots with your mum.

CHAPTER TWELVE

VERY GREAT BRITAIN

We live in, without doubt, the greatest country in the world. Sure, I've not lived in another one, so truth be told I've got no way of actually knowing if that statement's true, but if there's someone else out there that thinks differently and wants to nominate a better one, I challenge you to a duel! Well, not a duel per se, but I'm sure we could have a good old barney on Twitter instead.

What's this country of ours got going for it then? Well, to answer that, here's a rundown of what I think are the greatest things about Great Britain.

The Drinking Culture

Let's start things off with a biggun. No one drinks like the Brits. Our entire adult lives seem to revolve around the pub, whether you prefer to have a quick one after work, a lazy afternoon in a beer garden or a three-day bank holiday mega-binge. Personally I'd be up for all three, but if I had to choose one, it'd have to be a long, lazy afternoon in a beer garden in the height of summer. There's something about drinking outside in the sun us lot go crazy for. In most cities it's ridiculous; as soon as the sun's out you'll find every office worker tucking into a beer cramped onto the tiny two foot of pavement outside. To them it doesn't matter that they're inches away from traffic speeding past, as long as they get a bit of sun on their face while they drink that's all that matters.

Drinking is a real social thing in this country so it's best experienced while surrounded by a couple of your best mates, and even if none of your mates are around, the alcohol will soon fix that. You see, if we Brits have one weakness, it would be not being able to share our true feelings in public (stiff upper lip and all); however, get a few drinks into us and we'll be telling our entire life story to a total stranger.

'Nah, nah, mate, seriously, mate, nah, she ... she just grabbed ... she just grabbed my train ticket and ripped it up in my face ... and I was like ... o-oh! Someone's losing their virginity tonight!'

You'll probably recognise this most if you've ever been on a stag do. I love a stag do. Mainly because it combines two of my favourite things: meeting new people and drinking a bucket-load of booze. When on one, no matter how close you are to the groom, you'll rarely know everyone there – you might even find you know no one there except the groom – which is fine because you'll all be best mates by the time you even get to the second pub. Then by the third one you'll be inviting them on a weekend away with the family. And then by the fourth you'll be crying into their arms promising to name your next child after them.

Yes, we love a drink. But you may notice that in the last fifteen years or so, drinks have changed massively. I grew up during the alcopop boom. And if you're in your thirties, like me, you'll remember they were the perfect gateway drink for a teenager used to downing sugary drinks all day. The alcopops of choice back then were Smirnoff Ice, VK Ice, Hooch, Reef, Red Square, Lemonhead and Metz – which by the way was responsible for possibly the most terrifying advert there's ever been on British TV. If you haven't seen it, look up 'The Judderman' on YouTube and just imagine that coming on when you're home alone in the middle of the night. It's completely mental, mate.

These days alcopops are a dying breed, relegated to nightclub bars, probably because it's so dark inside people don't notice that what they're drinking is as gross a colour as Mum's mushy pea car. The trendy drinks at the moment are craft beers – which I absolutely love, although I'm sure like a lot of people, I'm judging them more on how hilarious their names are rather than the actual taste. Some of my favourite names for beers include: Hoptimus Prime, Beard of Zeus, Kilt Lifter and Yeastus Christ. If I ever came up with a beer I'd probably have to call it *See Ya Lager*. (Yes, I know it's a clunky pun, don't have a go at me. I mean, sure, it works written down, but say it out loud and you realise 'Lager' sounds nothing like 'Later'. Tell you what, tweet me if you can think of a better one.)

Until then, my drink of choice is definitely a Guinness. Yes, I'm a Guinness drinker, and not just on St Patrick's Day, either – I properly love the stuff. Maybe it's because it's so thick that when you drink it it feels like you're eating a proper meal at the same time. Also, speaking of St Patrick's Day, how English is it for our country to be like, 'Nah – I'm not going to make a fuss about St George's Day, I wanna celebrate the Irish one where you get off your tits on Guinness, thank you very much.' Even though, on paper, St George's Day should be way more exciting – it celebrates some geezer beating up a sodding dragon! But no, we'd still rather wear green and get totally rat-arsed instead.

Arron's foolproof hangover cure

I'm sure you can buy all sorts of medication to help cure a hangover, and the doctors will probably fill your head with nonsense about how to prepare before a night out and the exact ratios of water to alcohol you need to drink to make sure you don't wake up with a thunderous headache, but I promise you there's only one way to stop a hangover dead in its tracks. Here it is, my three-step guide:

1) Shit
2) Shower
3) Second Shit

I don't know how it works, it just does. Just remember that depending on the outcome of step three, you might need to repeat step two.

Music

Okay, this is impossible for anyone to disagree with: no one can argue that we have the best music in the world. Just look around you, you've got people like Ed Sheeran, Adele, Stormzy, Harry Styles and more absolutely dominating the charts.

This year Ed Sheeran's *Divide* album came out and did you know the week it was available he had nine songs in the top ten? That's just insane. I mean, Ed Sheeran? Sure his music is great, but he's a geeky little ginger kid from Suffolk. He wouldn't have lasted five minutes at Astor College and now look at him, he's so successful I bet he's getting more sex in a day than I've had my entire life. Speaking as someone who loves his tattoos, I have to admit,

Ed's got some pretty hilarious ones. All across his chest he's got an English lion, which sounds pretty cool and normal, then on his arm he's got a bloody Heinz ketchup bottle! And on his shoulder he's even got one that says 'LADZ ON TOUR'. I mean, come on, how awesome is that? All he needs is a 'See You Later' on his bum and his work will be complete.

And it's not just solo artists we've got. Britain's made loads of phenomenal bands, including Oasis, Blur, The Spice Girls, One Direction, Take That, Queen, Led Zeppelin, Coldplay, The Who, The Rolling Stones and the biggest-selling band in history, the Beatles. All from our lonely little island? That's insane.

For me, the peak of music was the Britpop scene in the '90s. Growing up, I was obsessed with Oasis. I reckon 'Half The World Away' has had a bigger effect on me than any other song in history. I remember a few years ago there was talk of this rivalry between One Direction and The Wanted like it was a big deal or something, but honestly there's never been a music rivalry like Oasis had with Blur. Whenever the bands released an album it made the news with the whole country desperate to find out who had done best. Some people thought the rivalry was all about The North versus The South because Oasis were from Manchester and Blur were from Essex; some people thought it was a battle of who you fancied more, Liam Gallagher or Damon Albarn; but to me it just came down to the fact that Oasis made bloody great songs. Don't get me wrong, I did really like Blur, too, but Oasis was everything to me in the '90s, as you can see from my Britpop top ten.

Arron's Britpop playlist

Here's my top ten '90s indie tunes. I suggest you pop on over to Spotify now and have a listen to them.

10) Ocean Colour Scene – 'The Riverboat Song'
9) The Lightning Seeds – 'The Life Of Riley'
8) Dodgy – 'Good Enough'
7) The Wannadies – 'You And Me Song'
6) Pulp – 'Disco 2000'
5) Blur – 'Parklife'
4) Oasis – 'Wonderwall'
3) Oasis – 'Rock And Roll Star'
2) Oasis – 'Whatever'
1) Oasis – 'Half The World Away'

If you gave me three wishes right now, then in a heartbeat the first one would be for Noel and Liam to put their differences aside and re-form for one last performance. Then, seeing as I've got two more wishes, I might as well make the second one be for them to ask me to join the band and play drums. And the third wish? Teach me how to play the drums, I guess!

Books

What do the kids love? *Harry Potter*. And what do the grown-ups love? *Fifty Shades*. Need I say more? No, but if you insist, how about Charles Dickens, Roald Dahl and that little geezer with the sick ruff, Billy Shakespeare? In fact, do you know who the second best-selling author in the country is? Jamie Oliver. I mean, fair play, he's cooking recipes from every other country in the world but this Brit's still bossing it. Hands down, the best chef in the world. All I need to do is learn the difference between the grill and the oven and I might finally be able to put all them cookery books to good use. (Love you, Jamie! x)

The Weather

People often say we've got terrible weather in this country, which if you ask me is bollocks. Yes it rains a lot but you know what, we also get baking hot days, too. Variety is the spice of life, my friend! You wouldn't honestly want it to be blazing hot all year round, would you? I bet you'd be begging for rain before you knew it. It's like food (everything's like food to me). Sure, you love cheesecake, but all year round you wouldn't want just cheesecake, would you?

What's even better than our actual weather is the fact that everyone is totally obsessed with it. In this country, we have three key topics of conversation:

1) what the weather is like
2) what the weather was like yesterday
3) what the weather will be like tomorrow

It's the ultimate ice-breaker, and the best way to fill some chat with one of those annoying people that makes you do all the work in a conversation.

The way we all react to slight changes in the weather is wonderful. If it's a couple of degrees hotter than normal, it's like, 'Right, here we go! Summer's here, let's get the shorts on!' Suddenly you go outside and everyone's wearing absolutely minimal clothing. Yes, women start wearing more revealing outfits, but they're not the only offenders. These days when it gets hotter the men out there react just as much, putting on the ridiculously short shorts and T-shirts with a neckline that plunges all the way down to their belly-button. As for me, when it gets hotter I'm just grateful that I've got a proper reason to wear my Ray-Bans. As they're part of my shtick, I sort of have to have them on me all the time, so when it's not sunny I look like a total Sunglass Wanker.[5]

And it happens the other way, too. As soon as it gets a little bit cold the country goes into a frenzy. The trains stop working, no one goes to work, no one goes to school, people rush to the shops to panic-buy food and we hunker down in our homes watching *Jeremy Kyle* until the weather picks up again. If we're this prepared for a bit of cold weather, just imagine how well prepared we'll be for the actual end of the world.

Movies

We're the home of James Bond! That's something to be proud of, right? I mean, okay, we don't have anything as massive as Hollywood over here, but if America's so great, why do they all come over here to film their movies? *Star Wars* is probably the biggest franchise at the moment (well, it definitely is for me and Alfie!) and they film that over at Pinewood in Slough. Yes, that's right, Luke Skywalker and the gang are fighting off The First Order just round the corner from *The Office*'s grotty Slough Trading Estate!

The other thing we've got are the best actors in the world. Those fancy Hollywood movie execs can't get enough of our lot. There's not many out there bigger than the likes of Tom Hiddleston, Idris Elba, Simon Pegg, Kate Winslet, Jason Statham, Emma Watson, Benedict Cumberbatch, Christian Bale, Tom Hardy, Eddie Redmayne, Daniel Radcliffe, Helen Mirren, Judi Dench, Orlando Bloom, not to mention our *Star Wars* idols John Boyega and Daisy Ridley. I still reckon there's room for one more out there in Hollywood, though; seriously, I can do action (I'm very good at getting

---

5 A Sunglass Wanker is the sort of person that wears sunglasses indoors or outside when there's absolutely no sun to be seen. I'm in no position to judge, though!

bundled into the back seat of a Chinese gangster's car), I can do comedy (well, I've got a catchphrase at least) and I can do romance (if your idea of romance is slow-dancing with a girl at a school disco for ten minutes and have her cry during the whole thing).

The Sense of Humour

We have the best sense of humour in the world. Humour is everything. It's what separates us from the animals (that, and the fact that we wear clothes and don't shit on the pavement). I've already chatted loads about my favourite comedy shows, but we've also got the best comedians in the world: Ricky Gervais, Peter Kay, Russell Brand, Michael McIntyre – these guys are megastars who fill out massive arenas and yet that's only scratching the surface of the talent in this country.

But the British sense of humour isn't all about arena-selling stand-ups, it's about you and me, mate. It's about all of us out on the street, on the bus and in the office. It's about that bloke on Twitter who makes a funny observation and suddenly they've got a thousand retweets. The whole country is brought up on a wicked sense of humour – we have a brilliant ability to take the piss out of each other and out of ourselves – but at the end of the day everyone knows it all comes from a good place. Some people call it being 'self-deprecating', but most of us call it by a much simpler name: banter. And no one does banter like Britain.

Banter is the foundation on which all friendships are made in this country. If you can't poke fun at your mates from time to time, and if you're not being poked fun at yourself, then I'm sorry but you don't have proper friends, mate. Get out there and find some new ones! I've got to meet loads of people doing what I do for a living, but I honestly reckon I can count my true friends on one hand. Everybody has different levels of friendship and in my case, right there at the top are my dear mates Bear, Hunter[6] and Richie Abbott; they're the greatest bunch of bastards a guy like me could ever wish for. I love you guys!

Now, the interesting thing about Richie (other than the fact that we obviously ran out of nicknames by the time we got to him) is that he is in fact the originator of the See Ya Later. Years ago, if we were out and having a few drinks (which, let's be honest, was all the time) he'd do this thing where he'd tell the whole table he was going for a piss before yelling, 'See ya later!' and walking off. It always made us laugh and lucky for me, Richie gave his blessing for me to adapt it for my videos. Actually, I wonder if maybe I should have got that in writing? Never mind, Richie wouldn't sue me. And even if he did, I'm sure it would just be banter.

The Language

Banter is also a good example of something else that's great about our country: the English language. I mean, sure, there's more people out there in the world speaking Spanish and a hell of a lot more people speaking Chinese, but none of them have a dictionary as good as us. We've got brilliant-sounding words like 'gobbledegook', 'gibberish' and 'codswallop', all of which are words that sound complete nonsense and also mean 'complete nonsense'.

And if you want more nonsense, look no further than London, where cockney rhyming slang is the most insane way of talking you'll ever find. Here's some traditional cockney rhyming slang that you might know already:

Apples and pears – stairs

---

6 That's two people, by the way. I don't know nobody called Bear Hunter, but I wish I did. That would be an incredible name.

'If you're looking for Arron, he's gone up the apples with some new girl and a Chinese.'
Dog and bone – phone
'You can't miss him, he's the bloke in the high street holding his dog up in the air.'
Boat race – face
'Yes, the one with the MASSIVE boat.'

Confusing, right? Here's a few more that I've made up for today's modern world.

Queen Latifa – FIFA
'Come round later and we can both have a play on Queen Latifa.'
Jason Bourne – porn
'She came in without knocking and caught me with my pants down looking at Jason.'
Judge Rinder – Tinder
'She's great, isn't she? We met through Judge Rinder.'

As well as cockney, the whole of Great Britain has some incredible accents and dialects. In no other country do people sound so different from town to town. We're only a small island, really, and yet we've got people speaking Cornish, Bristolian, Brummie, Scouse, Mancunian, Yorkshire, The Queen's English and Geordie to name a few – and that's just in England! You've also got Northern Irish, Scottish and my personal favourite, Welsh to really confuse the tourists.

And finally, can I just say, no one swears like the British. Yes, they're not very nice to be on the receiving end of, but my God some of our words are so bloody good to say. Obviously, as I mentioned earlier, I do my best not to swear, but even the biggest prude must watch someone like Malcolm Tucker swear and be like, 'Fair play, mate, what you just said then was a fucking poem.'

Manners

From one extreme to another. Yes, we can swear like a bunch of troopers but we've got the best manners of any country in the world. I mean, come on, we're the sort of people that would be casually walking in the street, get rammed into by a total tosser and still be the ones saying sorry!

From a very early age we're all taught to be humble, which is a great trait if you ask me. It's drummed into us because the last thing any one of us wants to hear is someone banging on about how great their life is. 'Ooo, you passed your driving test, well done', 'Ooo, you got a promotion at work, no one cares', 'Ooo, you got an A for your school project, go talk to your mother, maybe she'll give a damn.' It's not that we don't like other people to succeed at things, we just can't stand people talking about it.

We're so humble as a nation that it's impossible for us to take compliments. Even if someone says, 'Oh, that's a nice shirt, is it new?' we have to respond by going, 'What, this old thing? No, I've had it for ages.' Even though it's clearly got those fresh-from-the-packet creases and a label hanging out the back.

For those people that don't want to appear like they're boasting but still want to tell the world how great their life is, the last few years has seen the rise of one of the best and worst things of all time. I'm talking about the Humblebrag.

Humblebragging is basically when someone tries to say something amazing about themselves while hiding it inside a sentence that also makes them look like they're having a terrible time. When you hear somebody say one, it's a real thing of beauty – and they have to be called out on it immediately. If someone around you lets out a humblebrag, you cannot under any circumstances let it go without ripping into them! If you need help identifying them, here are a few examples:

Man, it's really difficult to get on with your workout when everyone keeps stopping you after each set to say how cut your arms are looking.

I think it's pretty patronising how people at work keep telling me what an amazing job I'm doing.

Buying a house is so stressfull!!! >(>(>(

God, ten people have told me my hair looks amazing today. What's so wrong with it all those other days, people?

Arrrrghhhh! Why do they make it so difficult to park a Lamborghini!

I've been flicking through all the likes on that last post of mine and now I've got really bad cramp in my thumb #prayforarron.

America is probably the total opposite of Britain, because while we always support the underdog and are almost sorry for when things go right for us, in the good ol' US of A, everything's great, and the only thing better than being great is talking about being great. If someone mentions something good about themselves to a fellow American they'll react by going, 'WOOO! Good job, Brad! You're amazing!' They love winners over there, while over here we love losers. Maybe that's why you bought this book of mine? (Okay, you got me – that's a humblebrag right there!)

Manners are sort of like social rules, and as a country that's a real stickler for rules, it's great to see fellow Brits react when people disobey them. We'd never dare confront someone or kindly correct them when they were doing things wrong. No, in Britain, if you step out of line you're going to be on the receiving end of something far more brutal: a tut.

Stand on the wrong side of the escalator and you'll get a particularly big tut. Get our order wrong in a restaurant, and you might be punished with an eye-roll. And the absolute worst for any Brit: step in front of us in a queue and you may well be hit with a tut, an eye-roll AND a humph. 'I didn't want to have to do that to you, but you forced me!'

Okay, okay, I've been a massive hypocrite here, I'm sorry. I've just said one of the great things about Great Britain is how humble we all are while writing a massive chapter about how great my country is. That's not very British, is it? Let's just put it down to me being patriotic, shall we? I reckon everyone should be proud of where they come from. Also, yeah okay, hands up, I guess there's still a few things that aren't really all that great about our country.

First of all, the place has been tearing itself to pieces ever since this Brexit bollocks. However you voted, it's managed to turn us all against each other and that's just not right. We're too busy focusing on the negatives, and not enjoying the one great positive to come out of Brexit. I'm talking about our country's stubborn refusal to say two words: British Exit. No, we couldn't possibly be expected to go around saying British Exit, so we came up with the phrase Brexit instead. Why? Because it saves time and also because you know what? It's just downright cooler. Bravo, Britain.

Here's some other 'Brexits' that are important in a modern world where people are too busy to be expected to have to say two words instead of one.

GREGSIT

Absolutely nothing to do with Brexit, this. Or Grexit even. It's simply the act of eating in at Gregg's. For some people this is a life-or-death decision, especially if, like me, you find it impossible to wait until you get home before breaking open that twelve-pack of Yum Yums. Plus there's no one to have to explain yourself to when you eat them all and refuse to share any. Well, no one except your conscience, and the eight or so people looking disapprovingly at you while waiting for their paninis to heat up.

JEGGINGS

Jeans plus leggings, this one. Not to be confused with skinny jeans. Jeggings are impostors and should be made illegal, they're so bad.

FRENEMY

Everybody knows this one. This is when someone appears to be your friend but secretly they're your enemy. It's a phenomenon more associated with girls than boys, mainly because I don't think blokes have the brain capacity to pull it off. Boys, if you want to understand it more it's basically that bit in *The Godfather* when he goes, 'Keep your friends close, but your enemies closer.' Which I guess is the beginner's guide to being a frenemy. My mantra is slightly different. I say, 'You'd rather have a friend with two chins than two faces.'

BROCOLATE

Like me, do you like to tuck into a Breakfast Chocolate? Don't listen to the nay-sayers. Just because it's only 8 o'clock in the morning doesn't mean it's a crime for you to chew away on that Double Decker. Mornings are tough, which is why I always keep one stitched inside my jacket for emergencies.

Of course I don't.

I keep two.

HANGRY

This means you're hungry/angry. It's what I feel each day if I haven't had my Brocolate.

*

But Brexit isn't the only thing that's been putting everyone on a bit of a downer lately. It seems every day you turn on the news and there's another excuse to say 'sod this' and go back to bed for a month or two.

But it's nothing more than a bump in the road! We can't forget what a cool fucking country the UK is. I know that whatever problems we have we can fix them. We're a country built on unity, love and kindness. I mean, just look at the NHS. There's nothing in Britain that shows just how much heart we have more than the National Health Service. Whatever's wrong with you, you can walk into your local hospital or doctor's, get treated and walk away without being asked for a single penny. Whatever your reasons for being unwell, they won't judge – even if it's something as idiotic as breaking your collarbone while showing off on a hoverboard for your latest Vine (true story).

So in summary, Britain is really fucking great.

But not *too* great, because as we've learned, no one likes a show-off.

CHAPTER THIRTEEN

DONALD TRUMP

He's a bit odd, right? He always makes me hungry. Probably because his hair looks like candy floss.

LADS ON TOUR!

Okay, one of the great mysteries of Great Britain is how other countries still like us, despite the fact that for the most part, we're total dicks when we go abroad. The most blatant example of this is during your average lads' or lasses' holiday. We're talking Ibiza, Magaluf, Faliraki, Ayia Napa, Kavos . . . maybe you've been on one, in which case you know exactly what I'm talking about. Lads' holidays are the perfect opportunity for young people to unwind after a tough year studying for exams. They're also a perfect opportunity to get pissed and absolutely destroy a small island in the Mediterranean.

If you watch one of those TV programmes like *Sun, Sex & Suspicious Parents* or *Ibiza Weekender*, they'd have you believe that you're basically getting laid every minute of every day, and as someone who's been on one of them, I can confirm that that is totally, 100 per cent, absolutely not true.

I went on a lads' holiday to Magaluf back in 2006 and it was probably one of the biggest disappointments of my life. Eighteen of us went who were all mates from college, and for the entire time we were there not one of us had sex. When we got there, we were so keen to get on it that as soon as we arrived at the hotel we dropped our bags off in the lobby and went straight into town. I say town, if you've ever been to Magaluf it's pretty much one or two streets lit up with bars. Along those streets are what's called promo girls who are trying to bribe you into one of their bars with a free shot (which is basically Ribena in a tiny cup). Yes, our first impressions of Magaluf weren't amazing but it didn't matter – we were there for a laugh and were optimistic about the week ahead, until we were walking towards our third bar of the night and a police car rolled up beside us. We were just minding our own business when they got out of the car and pepper-sprayed us all in the face! Then they drove off and left us rolling about in a blind mess. Welcome to Magaluf, lads! I promise you, we didn't do anything to deserve it but, like I said, us Brits abroad have a reputation, so maybe it was just a pre-emptive strike from the Spanish Five-O. To cap off a brilliant first night, when we got back to the hotel lobby we discovered that one of us had had their phone nicked from their bag. We decided against getting the police involved – we weren't exactly on good terms.

Not exactly the wild first night we were promised on this lads' holiday. It was too much for two guys, who decided to fly back the very next day. They didn't miss out on much, like I said; not one of us had any luck with the ladies and we just spent our time getting horribly drunk in the evening and more horribly sunburned in the daytime.

It was awful, but at least we can laugh about it now, which is another very British thing.

One of the most mental times abroad for me was a few years ago when I was asked to take part in a TV show for BBC3. The programme was called *Stupid Man, Smart Phone* and starred the hilarious comedian Russell Kane. In each episode, Russell was paired up with an online celebrity and the two of them had to undertake an insane journey in remote parts of the world armed only with their smartphones. Every episode was great (add it to your watchlist!), and for my episode, Russell and I were flown out to Marrakech, Morocco. My entire stay there was a time I would never forget, but on one night in particular, I experienced love, laughter and absolute terror all in the space of a few hours. That was the only night in my life where I've genuinely feared for my life.

For starters, Morocco was unlike anywhere I'd ever seen before. It's a beautiful part of the world; wherever you are in Marrakech you can smell the incredible local food they cook and you can always hear the commotion of people trading in the market, and every building you look at is crawling with history; seriously, guys, they all look like they were taken straight out of Disney's *Aladdin*. However, it could also be one of the most intimidating places I've ever been to. Folkestone has its moments, but it's got nothing on Morocco. I'm not saying the locals were unfriendly, they were great, but it always felt like we were treading a fine line and if we pushed our luck they would set Jafar onto us in a second. To be fair, I'd probably be the same if these two blokes rocked up with their sunburns, their loud, sarcastic voices and a camera crew.

The challenge Russell and I faced was to escort a camel from a market in the centre of Marrakech out to a drop-off in a place called Aït Benhaddou, which happened to be located across the freaking Sahara Desert. This was tough, and we were pretty useless at it to be honest. Russell and I wasted most of the first day trying to get Nathan out of the bloody market (Nathan was the name we gave our camel, by the way). The market was packing up for the night and we'd only moved about twenty metres! We ended up trading Nathan in for a little cow instead who was much easier to budge. Yes, we knew it was probably going to be an automatic fail, but it would have made for better telly than us two just arguing with a camel on a busy street corner for two days.

The night I want to talk about, the night of absolute terror when I actually feared for my life, was right towards the end of the challenge. We had made it to the desert and were marching through dry, dusty and rock-hard ground towards our target. We were tired, we were lonely, our feet ached like a son of a bitch and we were scared. Dehydration was already setting in and if that wasn't what was going to kill us, the wildlife certainly would have. We were warned about how dangerous the desert became at night by our SAS guide. Yes, you don't see him in the show but we had an SAS guide there with us. You might think that makes us cheats, but you know what, it wasn't as comforting as you'd think it would be. For starters, his name was Woody. Woody? The cow had a more macho name than that and she was called Helen. Also, having an SAS expert with you just adds to the tension. Woody was a constant reminder that our lives were in danger, which only made things worse. So there we are, Russell, me, Helen and Woody hiking through the barren landscape of the Sahara Desert towards some remote desert city that was nowhere in sight. Then, as the sun started to set, we heard the sound. Drums.

Drums are never good. Never in a movie do people hear drums, turn round and go, 'Ooh look, it's that lovely fella with one arm off of Def Leppard.' No, it means a marauding army like in *Lord of the Rings* or some evil geezer strapped to the back of a monster truck like in *Mad Max* – even that *Whiplash* movie about drum school had it's scary moments. Don't get me started on *Jumanji*. Drums meant danger, and this danger came in the form of a cluster of tents coming into view on the horizon. Smoke was rising from them and the drums were beating heavy and threatening from the same direction. Woody was the first to spot them.

'Stay here,' he warned, and went on ahead to make contact.

You don't see any of this in the show, I assume because they thought showing the SAS man coming to our rescue would undermine our bravery. Which of course was totally non-existent.

From where I stood it didn't look like he made a very good first impression; he was clearly arguing with one local before he was persuaded to go inside. Thank God for Woody, I thought, I'm sure he'll have the locals onside in no time. But this was clearly not the case, as fifteen minutes later he was still there. 'Oh my God they've killed him,' I thought. 'Russell, Russell, they've killed him. They've killed Woody!'

Russell was a rock. He had more faith in the Special Air Service than I did, and was not surprised when another ten minutes or so later, Woody emerged from the campsite and retreated back towards us.

'They're not happy we're here,' he said. 'They say this is their territory. We should get going.'

What we'd stumbled upon was a Berber tribe. This is a community of pre-Arab people that have lived in isolation throughout North Africa for thousands of years. Kitted out with heavy woollen robes and seriously angry faces, these people didn't look like the friendliest bunch of locals. In fact, they looked more like those Tusken Raiders from *Star Wars*, popping out from behind rocks getting ready to kick the force out of us. But we were in trouble either way, as we needed help getting water to stay hydrated. Despite Woody's warnings, Russell insisted on him and Woody going back to try and smooth things over with the Berbers – leaving me out on my own in the wild with just a small cow for protection. I was petrified.

Another five minutes goes by and Russell comes back insisting they now want to see me. I'm like, screw that, I don't want to be murdered in the middle of nowhere thank you very much. But realising I really didn't like the idea of dying of thirst, I went with him. Russell and I were there in the middle of the camp talking to these three dudes while all these other blokes were looking on. The longer we tried to explain ourselves to them, the more confused and pissed off they seemed to get, with more and more people getting involved. The discussion became pretty heated, and I started to piss my pants with what little liquid I had left in my body. Things were not looking good. Before you know it there's at least ten people gathered around all shouting in different languages.

But lucky for me, Russell cut off the tension when he opened up his little travel case and pulled out a peace offering; a diplomatic gift between nations, if you will. In fact, after Russell's gesture, their mood changed instantly and they started to welcome us into the group, which was a huge relief. What was this remarkable gift that brought peace to the desert? One of Russell's stand-up DVDs, that's what. And I don't know why they were so impressed, I definitely didn't see a DVD player knocking about.

The Berbers started to laugh amongst themselves it was like they'd suddenly been replaced by a totally different bunch of people. More of them started to come out of the tents. This wasn't a group of hard men. It was a family. There were mums, dads, aunties, uncles and kids of all ages. As we settled into one of the tents I began to miss my own kids like crazy. Luckily the whole point of the programme was giving us a smartphone with a constant signal, so at the earliest opportunity, I pulled out my phone and called the family. The second I heard Mia's voice my body just erupted with emotion and there, in the middle of the Sahara Desert, surrounded by total strangers[7] I sobbed like a baby. After the call, Russell gave me a massive hug and I cried some more. It was a surreal experience.

Shortly after, one of the local kids took a shine to my phone. He'd seen nothing like it before and wouldn't let me put it away without giving it a good inspection. I showed him some of the apps that my own kids love and his face lit up with joy – although considering

7 That moments earlier I was convinced were going to kill me.

how close his face was to the screen, that was mainly just the back-light. I opened up Netflix and put on *Peppa Pig*, feeling like some sort of Ambassador for Britain, bringing one of our finest exports to the natives of North Africa. The boy loved it. The others, not so much. Not at all, in fact. The tent filled with commotion and one of the local men knocked the phone out of the boy's hand. Yeah, turns out this whole camp are pretty hardcore Muslims, and they're not big fans of pigs.

'I think it's time for us to leave, Russell,' I whispered. We stood up to get out of there but the Berbers moved to block our exit. Oh boy. Then one of them started howling like mad.

'Russell, I don't suppose you've got another one of them DVDs in your bag, do you?'

The howling continued, then one man started growling and baring his teeth, then another was making ears with his hands. After an uncomfortable pause, it finally clicked. Turns out they weren't threatening us at all, and no, this wasn't some ancient Berber custom; they were actually warning us that now that it was night, the wolves were patrolling the desert. We had to spend the night there.

This wasn't your ordinary camping experience. Russell and I were shown to our room where everything smelt earthy, smoky and full of a musty ancient smell you'd normally expect to find in a museum. I call it a room; it was pretty much just the corner of the tent and where I lay down, the only thing separating me from the owner's face was a rug hanging from the ceiling.

That night, the temperatures dropped rapidly (it's bloody cold in the desert at night, my friend), so Russell and I had to layer ourselves up in these old, thick woollen blankets, including a sort of full-length Jedi hoodie that I could barely get my head into, let alone my whole body. Once I was settled and was able to block out the sound and smell of the bloke snoring into my face from the other side of the 'wall', I was in heaven. The situation was beautiful and I experienced possibly the most relaxing night of my life. There was a wide opening in the roof that meant I could look up and see the stars. You're probably thinking, 'Big whoop, Arron, I've been camping, we've got stars in Britain, remember?' Well these stars were unlike any I'd ever seen before, like thousands of clear white dots filling the sky. Seriously, it looked like a screensaver or something. I was as gobsmacked as a two-year-old Berber seeing *Peppa Pig* for the first time.

As I lay there, peacefully looking up at the stars, I played back the day's events in my head. Earlier that night I had witnessed some of the family eating dinner together. For those that watched the show, this was a proper meal, not the lizards we had to decapitate, skin, barbecue and eat; which by the way was even more horrible than it looked. When the family sat down to eat, there was no TV and no iPhones; there wasn't even a radio. That's not surprising, really, considering they live in the desert. All they could do for entertainment was talk to each other. It sounds corny, but watching that family having fun and enjoying being at the table together was beautiful and inspiring. It just looked right, you know? I was so inspired that when I got home I introduced a technology ban at dinner time. I was determined for us to live like the Berbers for the rest of our lives and to not spoil it by sitting in front of the telly watching *Pointless* with our plates on our laps. Sadly, the rest of the family didn't share the same epiphany as me and within a week we went back to the original routine. The only spiritual change the Crascalls have undergone is switching from *Pointless* to *The Simpsons* instead.

That night in the desert was probably the best sleep I've ever had and the next day, despite a long, long walk deeper into the desert, we made it to Aït Benhaddou with Helen intact. Yes, they were a bit miffed about Helen not actually being a camel like we had promised; apparently the fella we were taking her to needed one for camel rides, but I think we managed to persuade him that a baby cow ride would be just as much fun.

Morocco was a phenomenal experience full of every emotion. Whether or not it was an accident that we stumbled upon the Berber camp (there were a couple of times I reckon the production team had been plotting something horrible for us), my reaction to the situation was absolutely real. Perhaps Woody wasn't even an SAS hero. Perhaps Woody was an accountant at the BBC who fancied a break from the office. Of course in hindsight I was a total prat – the opportunity was incredible; I learned a lot about a beautiful culture, meeting an amazing group of men and women at that Berber camp.

I remain massively grateful to everyone on the team who got me to Morocco, but mainly I'm grateful to Russell Kane. I learned a lot about myself out there and what I was capable of, and in Russell I gained a real friend. So, cheers Russell!

My advice to anyone is to be adventurous. Don't settle for yet another lads' holiday or a week at the beach. Get out of your comfort zone and experience something new. Sod it, throw a dart at a map and go there. Wherever you go, just remember – even if you've got your back covered by ex-SAS, don't ever piss off the local police. That pepper-spray fucking hurts.

CHAPTER FIFTEEN

MI CASA

Despite how amazing the experience in Morocco was, I was very glad to be back home afterwards. The truth is a man's home is his fortress, and while Marrakech might boast the great pavilions of El Badi Palace, they're nothing compared to the great sofas of El Crascall Palace.

I live on a lovely terraced street in the heart of Dover. The houses are so tightly packed together that it's like whoever designed them got all his measurements wrong. The road outside is even more of a squeeze: you can just about fit a car down there with two or three atoms of space either side. I'd say it's the clearest evidence there is that we were much smaller all them years ago. That, or whoever designed the streets of Dover was off his tits.

There are few things in life as fascinating as other people's houses. It's my favourite bit of *Come Dine with Me* when they go tearing up the host's house like they were playing Pat Sharp's *Fun House* or something. What is it that makes us want to spy on other people in their homes? Do you ever have it where you're walking about at night and someone has the lights on but has forgotten to close the blinds, and you find it's totally impossible not to have a good old snoop? And no, I'm not talking about spying on people in their bedrooms or on the toilet – I'm not a monster, thank you!

I'm talking about people's kitchens and lounges, where you can stare as much as you like at their gaudy wallpaper, or marvel at the majesty of their 60-inch TV screen. You can't help it because you know it's totally risk-free; if they look out the window, all they can see is their own reflection. It's like a two-way mirror from a TV crime drama.

That's until they turn the light off, of course; then they instantly see you, pushed right up against the glass frantically writing down the serial number of that awesome TV.[8]

It may disappoint you to learn that my house is pretty ordinary; a pretty traditional two-up-two-down. It's only special to me, because it's where my family have grown up and where I've spent some wonderful years with Char. I wasn't joking though when I said my sofas were great. For starters they provide the perfect amount of comfort and support while in the two key lounge positions: sitting back watching TV and leaning forward playing video games. Next time you're shopping around in DFS, if a sofa can't provide both of these key features then it's simply not worth considering. And if it can't even provide one, then what the hell are you sitting on, a picnic bench?

The sofa is a sacred place in anyone's house, but it's nothing compared to the bed. The average person spends a third of their day asleep and over twenty-five years of their entire life between the sheets. Personally, it's often all I think of. In fact, my days pretty much always follow the same basic routine:

1) Wake up.
2) Stare at ceiling for twenty minutes.

8 Okay, I've just read that paragraph back. Yeah I really do just sound like a peeping tom, don't I? Sorry Mrs Barnes, turns out you were absolutely right calling the police on me. I promise it won't happen again.

3) Regret getting out of bed.
4) Yawn all day.
5) YES, back in bed.

This isn't me being lazy, by the way, this is science. Why else do you think our eyes water when we yawn? It's because we miss our bed so much it makes us sad enough to cry. You can't argue with that logic, mate. And now that I've written it here, you can go and tell people that 'fact', and when they say they don't believe you, you can confidently tell them that you read it in a book. SO THERE.

As for the actual quality of my bed, I can take absolutely no credit there. That's all Charlotte. Thanks to her, I'm always sleeping on fresh, clean sheets, a comfy, cloudlike duvet and more cushions than you'll find in the average Homebase. And before you sharpen your pitchforks and light your torches, I don't think cleaning up is a woman's job. I'm not sexist, I'm just completely incompetent. If I was left on my own I'm 100 per cent sure I'd be lying in my own filth instead. Growing up at home, I was so spoilt by Mum that she did literally everything. I didn't cook, I didn't wash up and I sure as hell never changed my bedsheets. Charlotte often jokes that I've been ruined and to be honest, I find it very difficult to argue with that. Honestly, I try and do my bit, but I can't even load a dishwasher without it going totally wrong. We both agree that it's for the best that I don't get let near any chores. Or at least, that's what I say.

It's all a matter of compromise. Charlotte accepts my inability to perform household tasks, and I accept her love of 'stuff'. You know, 'stuff'. I don't know if many other blokes out there have experienced the same phenomenon, but years ago when we first moved in together, overnight the house was transformed into an art exhibition. So much so that I could probably stand at the door and charge people to come and see all the incredible works of art. Fabulous pieces such as these . . .

Exhibit 31: *'Cluster of Tiny Drawers'*
Artist: Charlotte Crush
Medium: Junk in box
This work protests against the establishment. Order meets disorder as the typical purpose of each drawer is undermined by a stuffed tangle of any old random shit. Are the car keys in here? No, that would be too obvious. Instead, each small box contains hidden surprises such as a few snapped elastic bands, a single cuff link, a half-eaten pack of chewing gum, busted hairclips, a loose pork scratching, a forgotten Kinder Egg toy, a few euros that will never get used and a Regent Street sticker from an old McDonald's Monopoly promotion.

Exhibit 16: *'Massive Bloody Candle'*
Artist: Charlotte Crush
Medium: Flame on wax
This is an ironic piece, as despite its size and the fact it dominates the room, this candle is only lit one or two times a year. Considering how much a work of art like this can be worth, its lack of use is frankly a joke in itself. The artist will only ever light the flame to mask a particularly dominant scent released by the artist's boyfriend or perhaps to welcome the arrival of some very important guests such as a foreign diplomat, the Pope or that really good-looking ASDA delivery man she's got her eye on.

Exhibit 55: *'Bowl of Blue Pebbles'*
Artist: Charlotte Crush
Medium: Glass
At a distance, on the mantel this looks like an average bowl: simple, practical, elegant. Visitors are invited to step closer and see this work's true beauty – a collection of glass pebbles, each one subtly dyed cobalt blue. It resembles a bounty of treasure forged in the depths of the Pacific Ocean; which is good going considering a bag of them will only set you back a fiver at B&Q. Fans of this piece are advised to look out for other similar exhibits titled: 'Bowl of Random Shells', 'Bowl of Perfumed Bark' and 'Bowl of Stodgy Uneaten Rice Krispies'.

Actually, that bowl of uneaten Rice Krispies would be my contribution to the Crascall Museum of Art. You know what it's like – cereal has an optimum time in which it has to be eaten; leave it too long and it's a sloppy mess that's just not fit for purpose. I know what you're thinking; it's still no excuse for just leaving the bowl on the side, but how many times do I need to tell you? I'm the incompetent one! Other works of art courtesy of me include:

Exhibit 09: *'Orb of Tangled Man-Strands'*
Artist: Arron Crascall
Medium: Weaved hair
This living work of art, positioned stunningly beside the shower drain, represents inclusiveness. It daringly comprises material from everywhere on the artist's body. Head, face, back hair and pubes come together for a single, powerful

composition. You'll notice also how the artist has held the entire piece together using the lather, suds and scum from the past year's-worth of showers. Notice also how a welcome splash of colour is provided by the occasional balls of lint and belly button fluff. Genius.

Exhibit 11: *'Clothes Mountain'*
Artist: Arron Crascall
Medium: Polyester, wool and cotton
The notion of 'rejection' is explored in this installation, metaphorically and literally, as discarded items of clothing are seen artistically arranged around the general area of the dirty-clothes basket with very few actually *inside* the dirty-clothes basket. Notice the authentic smell, as if those boxer shorts were worn for five days straight before eventually being thrown behind the basket, where they've gone untouched for weeks.

Exhibit 99: *'The Infinite Disc Trail'*
Artists: Alfie, Mia and Evie Crascall
Medium: Performance
This is a site-specific piece of performance art exploring the themes of endurance and discovery. Participants are told to put the *Frozen* DVD into the DVD player. But the *Frozen* disc isn't in the *Frozen* case. Inside the *Frozen* case is *Despicable Me 2*, so is *Frozen* in the *Despicable Me 2* case? No, inside the *Despicable Me 2* case is *Toy Story 3*, and inside the *Toy Story 3* case is *Toy Story*, and inside the *Toy Story* case is *Ice Age* and so on and so on. The performance continues until participants find the end of the trail, or sack it off and go to the park instead.

It takes a lot of getting used to, living with your girlfriend. Like how all of a sudden the number of bottles in the shower multiplies by ten. And that's not all; every shampoo, conditioner, body wash, lotion and more is flavoured so that your shower now might as well be a fancy juice bar.

'Have you tried this Apple Zest & Pomegranate?', 'Why not finish it off with some Tea Leaf and Mint?' It wouldn't be so confusing if it wasn't for the fact they smell so damn tasty! You can't tell me that you haven't at some point thought about necking some.

Then there's the TV. Living on your own, you have free rein to watch what you want and record what you want. If I want to series-link *World Series of Poker* so that any time of the day I can get a shot of that 'just got in late from the pub' feeling, then I'm well within my rights to. However, as soon as she moves in you'd be lucky to record so much as a single flop,[9] seeing as the box will be constantly filled with repeats of *America's Next Top Model*, *Grey's Anatomy* and *Real Housewives of Cheshire*. I for one would love to see a *Real Housewives of Dover* – half of it would just be Char with her arms folded shaking her head disapprovingly at me.

It's different when you're living with your parents. It's in the genetic make-up of all dads to obsess over how much space is left on the Sky Plus box.

'We're up to sixty-two per cent! We're up to sixty-two per cent! Arron, I'm sorry but I had to delete all your episodes of *Bottom* to get us under sixty per cent.' Speaking of *Bottom*, living with your parents can be a real pain in the backside, and these days people have to wait ages before they can afford to move out and live on their own. But look at it another way: living with Mum and Dad includes a huge number of benefits. In fact, when debating

9 Little poker reference there for the hardcore card sharks that are reading.

what it's like living with your parents, you could end up writing the longest pros and cons list ever.

PRO: Mum's cooking. You can't beat dinner at Mum and Dad's, can you? If you're a food junkie like me, there really is no better place to live – unless of course you were able to start renting rooms in McDonald's.

CON: Always having to be told: 'This is not a hotel, you know, so stop treating it like one.'

PRO: Dads always make themselves available for lifts in the car, whether it's a quick trip to the train station or a late night pick-up from the arse end of nowhere because you dropped your phone while you got kicked out of the club and now have no way of booking that Uber.

CON: Always having to be told: 'I'm not a taxi, you know, so stop treating me like one.'

PRO: Not having to pay bills. It means you can spend money on more important things like treating your parents to a nice meal out, or saving towards a deposit for your own house so you can finally move out, or – if you're like me – spending it on a few hundred Ultimate Team packs to boost your chances of winning on the latest *FIFA*.

CON: Good luck getting near your Xbox when Mum and Dad have first dibs on what goes on the TV. Another episode of *Midsomer Murders* it is then, I guess. Oh, and don't think about going to your room to play – the 'rents will expect to spend some quality time with you in the lounge. And if you refuse, they just might refuse to tell you what they changed the WiFi password to.

PRO: Good luck with that, Mum and Dad! They barely

have enough technological know-how to open their
laptop, let alone change the WiFi password!

CON: Constantly having to help them with technology.
There's got to be a limit to the number of times a human
can say, 'Have you tried turning it off then on again?'

PRO: Simply spending time with the family. It really is a
treat just to enjoy each other's company.

CON: Overhearing Mum and Dad 'enjoying each other's
company' at bedtime. (Just keep telling yourself they
enjoy watching nature programmes in bed.)

CON: Having to live by their rules.

CON: No independence.

CON: No privacy.

CON: No freedom.

CON: Coming up with an answer to the question: 'What
the hell are you doing with your life, Arron?'

Sorry, looks like I got a bit carried away there. Jokes aside, I
loved the years I spent living with Mum and Dad and will always
be grateful for everything they did for me while I was there. I've
lived for a long time with them and I've lived with Char for many
years, too, but I've never properly lived on my own. If I'm being
honest, I don't think it's as good as it sounds. Don't forget, according to Char, I did so little housework growing up that I'm ruined.
Yeah, I'd be a mess if I lived on my own. I can't even work a tin
opener. Come round after a few weeks and you'll probably find me
super-skinny and calling the TV remote Wilson like I was Tom
Hanks in *Castaway*.

You know that feeling when you're on your own and you hear
a noise in the house? I'm the sort of person that will run upstairs
and barricade himself inside a fort I just made out of mattresses
and bed sheets. If I lived on my own I'm not sure I'd ever come out

of there. Remember that bit in *Home Alone*, when in order to fool the Wet Bandits into thinking he wasn't on his own Kevin built a party in the house with cardboard cutouts of people and loud music? It wouldn't take long before I would be doing the same, mainly for the company. My neighbours would either be thinking, 'Wow, that Crascall bloke sure has a lot of parties', or (more likely), 'The strange man next door is talking to his cardboard cutouts again, do you think we should call the hospital?' I think that's what I'd miss most about living on my own, having someone to talk to.[10]

Okay, here's a big advance warning, what follows is going to sound incredibly soppy, almost pathetic even. If you're sensitive to a bloke showing some sensitivity, then skip on to the next chapter . . .

To me, my home is my family. It's wet but it's true; I could be under the same roof I've been living under for years surrounded by the same pile of bricks, but if my family's not there with me, it just doesn't feel right. They say home is where the heart is and I think there's a lot of truth to that. Your heart might also belong to your family and you'll understand what I'm saying. Or it could belong to something else; like your friends, or a pet. It might not even be a living thing – hell, for a long time when I was a kid my heart belonged to my Mega Drive, but let's be honest, 'Home is where the Mega Drive is' doesn't have much of a ring to it.

10 Yeah, more like show off to.

CHAPTER SIXTEEN

FAMILY

I feel bad for making jokes about living with Mum and Dad in that last chapter. It would kill me if they thought I wasn't grateful for the years I spent living with them. I mean, yes, Char was right, Mum did 'ruin me' by making sure she was the one that did all the housework, but how many other mums are so caring they'd take cutlery up to your room to help you woo the girls you bring home? Not to mention pay for every one of your dates!

Mum is the most selfless person I know. She's always thinking about others and never shows any interest in herself. She's retired now, and rather than spending her spare time chilling out in the garden with a gin and tonic in her hand all day, she spends all her time volunteering for a local children's hospice. The work she does is incredibly inspiring and makes me so proud. I've been to the hospice where she works and it makes me so emotional to see the effect Mum and all the other volunteers have on these kids. And then, after giving up her time for those children, she still has time to be an amazing nanny for our three.

When I was young my mum slogged her guts out working in loads of pubs around Dover including top boozers the Cherry Tree and The Diamond. They're still knocking about today, but even if they weren't, all I'd need to do is close my eyes to picture them clear as a bell in my head just like they were back in the '90s. They were proper old-man pubs, the kind that stank of smoke, beer and salt and vinegar crisps. 'Old-man pub' couldn't be more appropriate, either as they were always full of blokes who at the time looked ancient to me and scary. These pubs were intimidating places; you walked in and all these old men with angry, craggy faces would just stare at you, not even looking away to take another sip from their tankards. Who could blame them? An eight-year-old boy had just walked in bold as brass, and this was not a place for kids. These days pubs have become real family joints; a place to get a nice meal together or have the little ones play on the climbing frames while Mum and Dad ignore them and have a drink in the beer garden in peace, but back then this was the home of the working man. I say working, I was in there after school most days and I don't know many jobs that let their staff out at 3.30 in the afternoon.

Because it was my mum, Cess Crascall, working behind the bar, whenever I walked in there I felt untouchable. Like I was a celebrity bowling in there. I was always well looked after by everyone and began my lifelong career of propping up the bar – only at that age, the Cokes I was downing had far less Jack in them. Of the two pubs, I always preferred meeting Mum at The Diamond. Sometimes me and my sister Amy could be waiting a long time for her to finish her shift, so the fact it had a pool table upstairs really helped pass the time – and ensured that no homework ever got done. The Diamond also had this box at the end of the bar that was full of rolls they were selling for 50p a pop. They were classic flavours like ham and tomato and cheese and onion (this was not the place for fancy fillers like prawn or avocado), and because I was Cess's son, I could tuck in to as many as I wanted. Downstairs in the basement of The Diamond was the kitchen. I'm told that a murder once took place down there, which is proper unsettling for an eight-year-old although looking back I'm pretty sure someone made that up to keep me out of there and make sure the only food I was nicking was the rolls.

Arron's top five sarnies

5. Cheese, Beetroot & Mayo (yes, okay, controversial I know, I'm just one of those guys that loves beetroot).
4. BLT (meat. Standard).
3. Chicken & Bacon (double meat. Double standard).
2. Seafood Mix (another unusual choice but hey, I live by the sea).
1. Cheese & Pickle (the undisputed king of the sangers. But absolutely has to be on thick-cut bread. And if you dare grate that cheese, I'll be putting that grater up some place really unpleasant).

She's a special lady, is Mum, and when you consider how as well as her shifts at the pub she also juggled working long hours at Tesco, she really did everything she could to provide me and Amy with an amazing childhood. Amy is a special case. She's five years younger than me and my only sibling. As I'm the only brother she's got, I've naturally fallen into the role of being both her chief tormentor and her chief protector. What that means is, while I love pulling pranks on her, if anyone else out there thinks they can mess with her, then they're asking for a world of pain from yours truly.

Seriously, my commitment to being Amy's bodyguard has put me into some pretty stupid situations. I remember once walking into the pub one evening to find Amy on her own, looking upset. Without a second thought I marched out of there to the pub over the road (there are a lot of boozers in Dover) where I found her boyfriend at the time hunched over a fruit machine giggling with his mates. 'Who does this prick think he is?' I thought to myself.

'Breaking my sister's heart then getting pissed with his mates in the very next pub while she's sobbing alone?' I dragged this clown away from the fruitie and back to Amy next door, running my mouth off at him as we went.

Turns out I'd massively read too much into the situation. Amy wasn't as upset as I thought, and the boyfriend had just lost track of time and was a little bit late meeting up with her. Yeah, my reward for trying to help the situation was an earful of abuse and a few thumps from Amy. Not for the first time the Crascalls put on quite an emotional display for the locals. Not that it bothered us; we were never afraid of telling each other what we thought, no matter who else was in the gaff.

But I can't help it; like I said, I'm a natural protector. If you think Amy's boyfriends had it bad, I feel for the poor blokes who even think about dating my two daughters. Right now Mia and Evie are three and one but when they become teenagers, and boys start sniffing around, the Crascall household will become a total war zone. I'll buy a couple of air rifles so that when boys come round, me and my mates could have the guns laid out on the kitchen table, polishing them when they arrive. I probably wouldn't even say anything, either; I'd just slide a questionnaire under their noses for them to fill in.

Arron's potential boyfriend questionnaire

Here it is. The ten very straightforward questions I will be putting forward to any male who thinks they might be entitled to dating one of my daughters.

1) Do you have a job?
   a) If No, how do you intend to provide for my daughter?

   b) If Yes, stop wasting your time and study for a proper career.

2) Where do you see yourself in ten years' time?
   a) A Lawyer.
   b) A Brain Surgeon.
   c) A million miles from my daughter because only one of the above is good enough for her.

3) Are you a virgin?
   a) If No, do you have a complete, detailed breakdown of all prior intimate engagements, along with a recent urine sample?
   b) If Yes, that's cool and all, but is that because there's something all the other girls know about you that my daughter doesn't?

4) Have you ever tested positive for any of the following?
   a) Herpes
   b) Gonorrhoea
   c) Chlamydia
   d) Crabs
   e) Unfaithfulness

5) Which of the following is the correct way to drive?
   a) Up to but not exceeding the speed limit.
   b) As slow as humanly possible.
   c) Not at all, because my daughter's life is precious and not to be risked inside your danger-wagon.

6) Do you love Alan Partridge?
   a) If Yes, move on to Question 7.
   b) If No, I'm sorry but that's an automatic fail.
   c) If you're thinking, 'What's Alan Partridge?' Start running. I'm going to give you a 30-second head start.

7) Which of the following do you think is the correct way to break up with someone?
   a) Over the phone.
   b) In a text.
   c) In person.
   d) Never, because you know that my daughter is an angel who is much too good for you and your pathetic little existence.
8) Do you honestly realise what you've let yourself in for?
9) I mean it, do you?
10) Seriously, why are you still standing there reading this? Did you not see me polishing my guns?

Okay, I'll admit it, I'm an over(ish) protective father. That's not a crime though, is it? Well, okay, I guess it will be a crime if I end up having to shoot one of them, but I'm sure I'll have good reasons that will stand up in any court. Maybe it's because he's so much older, I'm not as worried about Alfie. He'll have a questionnaire but it'll be a lot shorter. In fact, it will probably just have the one question: 'Are you actually interested, or are you going to turn out to be a bit of a prick tease and cry to him about other boys instead?'

On second thoughts, when Alfie gets older I think I'll do what my dad did which is to get a front row seat and watch him fumble his way to eventual success with the ladies. Good old Robbie Crascall knew what he was doing when I was growing up. Dad, by the way, is simply the soundest bloke a son could hope to have looking out for him. He's also the blueprint for a perfect man: for starters, he's practical. He can do all the important things you'd expect a dad should be able to do like wire a plug, build a shelf, bleed radiators, fix a leak, stuff like that. As for me, I've got zero life skills. Seriously, I have trouble cutting a slice of bread straight, let alone perform any sort of DIY. Dad also loves manly things like fishing and cars and football and pints (we have that one in common). But most importantly he's got a wicked sense of humour, which means we always have the biggest laugh when we're around each other.

There's plenty of banter amongst our family, especially when it's directed at Dad. In particular we love to give him a bit of stick about his height. If you saw him you'd never say he was short; he's about 5'7", 5'8", but because Mum's 6'1" he looks tiny next to her. What can I say? It's clear that, just like me, Dad wasn't afraid to punch above his weight (or height, I should say).

While Mum worked in the pubs, Dad spent his days running the warehouse at the local paper mill in Dover. I got to see him in action once when I did work experience there while I was still at school. They wouldn't let me work alongside him (that's cheating, apparently) so I had to watch from afar while I worked as an electrician. Which of course, I was useless at. With my total lack of practical skills all I'm saying is thank God there was a supervisor with me at all times. Otherwise I would have shocked myself a hundred times a day and almost definitely would have cut out all power in the entire mill.

Dad packed in the job when the company left Dover and set up in Germany instead. If Dad had gone with them I don't think I would have lasted long – I'm barely coping at English, I'm not sure my brain could cope if you threw German at me, too. Although I do really love Germany. Last year I visited Hamburg and had an amazing time: lovely people, lovely food, and also the cleanest city I've ever seen.

After Dad said see ya later to the paper mill, his next job was running customs checks on the Dover docks, making sure no one was trying to bring anything dodgy into the country. I always imagined it was like in some crime drama with him armed with a pistol, a flashlight and a pack of rowdy sniffer dogs trying to take down a drugs operation on the docks. Sadly, though, there were never any drugs busts, but he did once take down a big shipment of smuggled cigarettes and porn. Who smuggles in porn?? That's what the internet's for.

Mum and Dad have been together for thirty-four years and during that entire period I've not seen them argue once. Mum tells me the secret to their success is making sure they spend plenty of time away from each other. Sure enough, every week they always have their own 'me time': on Wednesday Mum has her night away playing darts with the girls, and on Sunday Dad gets his: playing skittles with the boys. I can see the appeal of throwing darts at a wall but skittles has always confused me. Sure, knocking the skittles over is fun but then you've got to pick them up after. Why would anyone do that when you can go ten-pin bowling and have a machine pick them up for you? And you can play some air hockey. Madness.

When it comes to romance in the Crascall family, the apple hasn't fallen far from the tree as I'm partial to the odd loving gesture or two myself. I recently took Char for a walk up to the top of the O2 in London, which was a great experience and very romantic. If you haven't done it, I recommend you do – you get loads of brownie points with the missus – but fucking hell is it tough. 'Walk' is an understatement. There are times when the climb is so steep you're practically crawling up a wall, so unless you're feeling particularly fit (or if you've recently been bitten by a radioactive spider) I suggest you park it and take the other half out for a meal instead. The other thing about climbing the O2 is that when you're on your way up it's basically a massive long trampoline. Sure I'm carrying a bit of weight, so on my way up the thing was bouncing like crazy. Turns out even though it's built just like a trampoline, the staff really don't like you treating it like one. The Sherpa bloke that took us up started having a go at me and I'm like, 'Mate, I can't help it! Believe me, we are *really* high up and I *definitely* don't want to get bounced off this thing!'

When we got to the top, the views were spectacular. It really is a beautiful way to see London, especially on this occasion because it was starting to get dark and you can start to see all the buildings lighting up in front of you. Char was loving it, totally focused on spotting all the different parts of London she recognised. I'd had this moment planned for months and tonight, I was ready to make my move. I was finally ready to ask Charlotte to be my wife. So there, on the top of the O2, with her distracted by the view, I bent down on one knee behind her. She turned round just in time to see me pulling out the ring box before I asked, 'Charlotte Crush, will you marry me?'

Okay, I'm not going to tell you what she said next. Just park that thought. Instead I'm going to tell you something else fascinating about the O2. You see, when you climb it, you have to leave all your stuff in a box. Everything. They don't want anyone going up there with stuff in their pockets or in a bag even, because apparently all it takes is for you to drop a coin and it can pretty much kill someone on the ground if it lands on them. This ban on stuff is a great way to protect the people below but threw a massive spanner in my planned proposal. But I didn't let a silly rule like that get in the way. You see, in order to get this ring up to the top, I craftily smuggled the ring box into the most secure place I could: my boxers.

I don't know if you who are reading this are married or engaged and have already gone through the whole proposal thing. Maybe you're single but you've already got your ideal scenario in mind. But I think everyone can agree, the one thing you don't expect your potential fiancée to say after you propose to them is:

'Did you just pull that from out your pants?'

There were probably fifteen or so people up there that evening, and after Charlotte said that, they all started absolutely pissing themselves. Then Char and I started laughing. Everyone found the whole situation a bit hysterical. And then she said it:

'Of course I will, you complete idiot.'

And that was that. Char put on the engagement ring (despite where it had been), we both had a bit of a cry and the fifteen strangers up there gave us a round of applause.

Thank you for saying yes that day, Charlotte. You are one in a billion and I owe you everything. Only you have the strength to put up with an idiot like me. You've always been incredibly supportive, even when I came home one day and said, 'You know what, I'm going to quit my job and post videos on Facebook full time for a living.' You never once tried to persuade me not to. I really am too lucky to have you, and while I'm sure there will be the occasional time when I do something so idiotic that for a split second you might regret saying yes, I promise I'll do everything I can to prove to you that it was the best decision you'll ever make in your life. Love, Your Arron x

CHAPTER SEVENTEEN

WORKING 9 TO 5ish

Of all the people making a living doing stupid things online, I'm probably one of the oldest, if not definitely the oldest, out there. All the other people you subscribe to online have likely built up their following before they've even left school, which means it's probably the only job they've ever had (lucky bastards). I'm sort of the complete opposite. Over the years I've probably had every type of job you could imagine. Let me take you through the old Arron Crascall CV; it's pretty extensive, and I'm not going to lie – leaving those jobs wasn't always necessarily my decision.

Like many people do in this country, I became a working man when I was still at school. As if slogging my guts out in the classroom from Monday to Friday wasn't bad enough, I'd also chosen to give up my weekends, too, just so I had a bit of extra money to waste on pints, video games, pints, CDs and more pints. Okay, I never really 'slogged my guts out' at school, and yes, I don't think I ever really 'slogged my guts out' in any of my weekend jobs either. But it really baffles me that any teenager would willingly give up their precious weekend just so they had a little bit of extra pocket money to waste down the pub.

My first job was at fourteen, working at the local Co-op as a shelf stacker. If anyone's done this sort of job before you'll know it's possibly the most boring work you can imagine, constantly moving backwards and forwards from the back room to the shop floor, spending all day filling the same shelves. Always having to apologise for being in the way, always being interrupted by customers looking for eggs when they're clearly already standing in the middle of the sodding egg aisle. Then you get your arse handed to you by some jobsworth supervisor because those bottles of ketchup you just spent the last half an hour putting out aren't all facing in PRECISELY the same direction.

The absolute worst thing about working in a supermarket, though, is that when you get hungry it feels like torture. Imagine you're totally starving, you're four hours away from your next break and all that time is spent handling packets of Jaffa Cakes that you're not allowed to open. Then when your break finally comes around, you're so hungry that all the money you earnt that morning is spent on food. Like I said, it's excruciating work. Which is why when I turned fifteen I eagerly left to discover an entirely new career . . . stacking shelves in *Iceland*. If you thought stacking shelves in Co-op sounds bad, imagine doing the exact same job while totally freezing your nuts off in every aisle. Not fun, let me tell you.

After Iceland, I started my long-running career in the food industry, beginning at the very top: chief washer-upper at The Plough Beefeater in Dover. I was utterly useless. Like Char said, I've never been good at household chores, and getting paid for what is essentially one massive household chore didn't make me any better. They could have hired a chimpanzee and they would have done a better job than me. I really hit the big time, though, when I left and started work at the Golden Palace Chinese takeaway. It was my first job since leaving school, so it was important for me to start earning some good money. Actually, getting paid ANY money would have been good. The whole time I was there

I didn't see a single penny; instead it worked out better for both of us to pay me with free Chinese food, which, as a young man obsessed with Sweet & Sour Chicken Balls, I gladly accepted.

After the Chinese I worked at a curry house, in what was probably a world record for the shortest time in one job. There I lasted an incredible four hours. I was working in the kitchen (a big step up from my washer-upper days but still a long way off from becoming Dover's answer to Gordon Ramsay) and was part of a sort of production line getting ingredients ready for someone else to do the proper cooking. I was basically paid to chop onions. That evening, on my very first shift, I learned two very important things about working in a curry house: 1) There's a whole lot of onions in Indian food and 2) restaurant knives are *a lot* sharper than normal knives.

That's right, I went and cut myself pretty bad. Like I said, I was a long way from Gordon Ramsay. It was my own fault; they taught me how to use a knife, and warned me a lot about how dangerous the knives were, but I was a little cocky and a lot useless and thought I could chop as fast as the chefs do on TV. I was chopping very fast for a beginner, but chopped very fast right into my left hand. When it happened, I didn't even feel a thing, that's how sharp the knife was. But I sure as hell noticed when the blood started pouring. My first thought was, 'That's weird, I don't remember these being *red* onions', and then it properly gushed, I mean like posh-fountain levels of gushing. I looked at my hand and I just shrieked; the cut was so deep I could see white. I still don't know what that white bit was; it could have been a bone, it could have been a tendon, it could have been a bit of poppadum that slipped in. Whatever it was it was very bad, and I ran around the kitchen in a panic, my blood spurting into every single pot, pan and onto every surface there was, contaminating absolutely everything. All the food and utensils were completely spoilt. They had to close early and chuck out a lot of food. That night I cost them a whole heap of money so it wasn't surprising that the next day I walked out of A&E and into the Job Centre.

The best jobs in the world

If I was asked to describe what I do for a living, I would say I was either a comedy performer or a professional idiot. Whatever you call it, this is hands down my dream job, and I'll always be grateful for having this opportunity.

However, there are still plenty of other great jobs out there, and if it all ended tomorrow, you can bet I'll be dusting off my CV for some of these genuine jobs out there.

LEGO Builder

If only I could go back in time and tell my eight-year-old self that he could make a living building things with Lego. I would have stopped wasting time going to school and put all my efforts into plastic bricks.

Tea Taster

Imagine getting paid to drink tea? Sounds amazing, right? The job requires you to drink 300 cups of the stuff every day, which for a tea obsessive like me is brilliant. Although if you're the sort of person that struggles to get to sleep after a single cup of tea, let alone 300, maybe the next job is better.

Professional Bed Warmer

No joke, there are people out there that will pay you to lie in their bed and warm them up before they turn in. Weirdos, if you ask me. Who wants a warm bed? There are few things nicer than the cold side of your pillow.

Water Slide Tester

This is insane. Getting paid just to ride water slides and tell people what you think of it. Sign me up, mate.

Island Caretaker

Some guys in Australia will pay you over £70,000 to live on and look after an island on the Great Barrier Reef. This is utter paradise, plus if Tom Hanks in *Castaway* is anything to go by, it's a good way to lose a bit of weight.

After 'the onion incident', I never worked in a restaurant again, and soon found work at Argos. I always used to think there was something quite magical about shopping at Argos. You turn up, tap a number into a machine and not long after, your item comes out from the back. It's like the world's biggest vending machine. Well, it might seem magical for the customers, it sure as hell isn't for the poor bastard in the back who's got to run around and find everything. I'm not exactly built for running or climbing, so I soon learned that working out the back of Argos wasn't exactly the career for me, so I moved a couple of shops down the high street and got a job as the suit manager in Burton's. That was fine; there was less running around and a lot less climbing but my God, it was boring, and I've never been much of a suit person, so I don't think I was very convincing at selling them. That job was as much of a bad fit for me as the three-piece they had me wearing, so I soon moved even further down the high street to an independent record store.

The record store gig was fantastic. I loved it. I'd work there during the day, then most nights and weekends I was DJing at various bars in and around Dover. I was finally putting what I'd learned at school to good use! All those years spent skiving off to play jungle music at Stuart's were paying off. The two jobs together were a perfect fit. I mean, sure, I preferred DJing, but working in the record shop was sort of like revising – I'd get to listen to all the latest music and then when I wasn't serving customers I could work out my sets for that weekend. I love DJing. Back then I was in my twenties and it did a good job of fuelling my craving for attention. I always knew I wanted to perform for a living, which is why I was so unsatisfied with every job I'd had up until that point.

Unfortunately the record store eventually closed and I was left to get by on just my DJ gigs – which you may not be surprised to learn ain't a whole lot of money. Before long I was in desperate need of a proper job, and when a big opportunity came along, I had to say yes – even though the schedule meant I had to put my career goal of becoming a world famous DJ on hold. And I'm very glad I did, because if I hadn't said yes to that job, I never would have got to know Charlotte, and without her I wouldn't be where I am now. The job was working the bar for P&O ferries and involved travelling across the English Channel six times a day pouring drinks for 1,500 people a trip and nearly 10,000 people a day. It was tiring work, but it made me. Spending my days interacting with that many people really helped boost my confidence. Which, by the way, when your current job involves going up to strangers in the street and asking them to take your hand and dance with you, is the most important thing to have.

Working on a ferry is an odd lifestyle. People always ask, 'How do you cope with the seasickness?' But honestly, if you spend as much time as we did on the water, that all goes pretty quickly and you end up suffering from something way worse: land sickness.

Seriously, you're so used to the rocking of a boat that when you eventually get on dry land, the stillness makes you want to puke. Puke by the way is something you get very used to working on a ferry. Fortunately I was never on 'clear-up duty', but I remember one occasion when a little old lady looked lost. Being the helpful guy I am, I leaned in to ask if I could be of any assistance and she paused, looked me dead in the eye for five seconds and then puked right in my face. I'm talking proper *Exorcist* levels of puke. Like if puking was an Olympic sport, she'd be representing Team GB for sure, mate.

There were two boats going back and forth across the Channel: the *Pride of Dover*, and the *Pride of Calais*. I worked on the *Pride of Calais* on what was known as 'green watch'. Char was a stewardess on 'red watch', which meant that even though we worked the same boat, we did opposite shifts and never really saw much of each other. I'd actually known Char from a while before. She had gone out with a friend of mine and when we realised we both worked the same boat, we started texting each other. I guess in a way green watch and red watch were like rival gangs, and our relationship was like something out of *Romeo & Juliet*. Eventually the texts increased in number and got increasingly flirty, and before long we were in a proper relationship. It couldn't have come at a worse time, though, as around the same time I lost my job.

The only downside to my time working with P&O (beyond getting puked on by old ladies) was that I liked to work hard but play harder. There was a big social vibe while I was working there, and I was always desperate to socialise with my co-workers because it was often the only time green watch and red watch mixed and my only chance to spend time with Charlotte. Eventually the constant partying started to affect my work and I ended up coming to an agreement with my bosses that I wasn't quite cut out for it and left.

This is where I will always be hugely grateful to Char because this was when my long stretch of unemployment began. We hadn't been together very long and already Char was paying my way. The only jobs I could find were working nights in Tesco, behind local bars and performing maintenance on the railway lines. (That's right, I was trusted to fix the rail lines! Think about that next time you hop on your train to work. Perhaps you're on a train right now while you're reading this – bet that fills you with a lot of confidence!)

Eventually, at the age of thirty-one, I landed my last-ever 'proper job'. For nearly three years I worked at a William Hill taking bets. It is hands down the most depressing job I've ever had. It's horrible work. Sure, it's special when someone wins big and you get to share in their joy. But joy doesn't come very often to people at the bookies. More often than not, people come in and blow away a lot of money on stupid bets, and I mean a lot of money. It was honest work but took a massive toll on my emotional state. You literally saw people's lives go up in smoke right before your eyes. I lost count of the number of times people would come to me in tears begging for a second chance as they just spunked their life savings or their kids' uni fees up the wall. You'd come in in the morning and just be on the receiving end of constant abuse from desperate customers all day.

It was there, behind the bullet-proof glass of William Hill that I decided enough was enough. It gave me all the motivation I needed to focus my efforts on my true calling: making stupid videos. I started on Snapchat, filming the odd funny on my phone to amuse my friends, but more importantly to bring some joy to an otherwise depressing day. The reaction was great, but because it was Snapchat, once my videos were seen, they disappeared. Then my mates told me about this thing called Vine, saying I had to start putting my stuff on there instead. My friends enjoyed it, then they started sharing my videos with their friends, then they started sharing them with their friends, and so on and so on. It was unbelievable how quickly the numbers were going up. Hundreds became thousands, thousands became tens of thousands and then hundreds of thousands and then millions! It's totally ridiculous. I was just a normal bloke from Dover, and all of a sudden I was starting to get recognised in the street.

It took about two years from when I first started doing my videos to when I was getting enough views to be able to quit William Hill and become a full-time professional idiot. I still can't quite believe it all. I've been incredibly lucky, but you know what, I'm also proud to say that I have done my time working some pretty rubbish jobs before getting here. There's nothing quite like cutting your hand in half in a curry house restaurant or getting puked on by a stranger on a ferry to make you appreciate what you've got when you've got it.

I hope that, as a completely average bloke who's somehow found a way to do his dream job for a living, I can inspire some of you lot out there to chase down your dream, whatever that might be. If you asked me for some advice, I wouldn't know what to say other than do what I did and get yourself a horrible job you hate and maybe that will inspire you to pull your finger out and pursue something you enjoy doing instead! Also, remember I got into this game relatively late. Whatever your situation, it's never too late to say 'screw this' and start doing something completely different that you enjoy instead. And don't forget what my man Confucius says: 'Choose a job you love, and you will never have to work a day in your life.' Or was it Alan Sugar? I can't remember.

CHAPTER EIGHTEEN

PROCRASTINATION HELL

Writer's block. What a bastard that is. I'm the sort of person who forgets what he's going to say when in the middle of a tweet, let alone in the middle of a bloody book. It's a massive frustration, and isn't helped by the fact that I am so easily distracted.

This chapter is dedicated to my procrastinating habits: the things that have been occupying my time when what I should really be doing is pulling my finger out and actually writing! If you've ever had to do anything that requires a level of self-discipline, whether it's a presentation for work or revision for an upcoming exam, I'm hoping you can share some of the frustrations I'm facing. Unless, who knows? Maybe I'm the only person out there with an attention span shorter than a gnat's.

The biggest problem is social media. Social media is too bloody addictive! Every minute you're not looking at your phone, you're missing a minute of what's happening on Facebook, a minute on Instagram, a minute on Twitter and a minute on Snapchat. So for every minute that goes by in real life where you're not on your phone, that means there's another FOUR minutes of social media time to catch up on. And even when you are on your phone, by the time you've gone through all your socials you're ready to start again from the top. If you suffer from as much social media FOMO as I do, you'd be with me in saying you could go your whole life doing the same social media cycle:

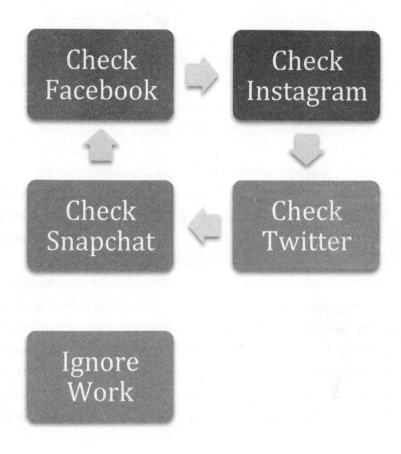

For the most part I've been writing at home, which is where I am right this second. I'm currently sat at the kitchen table, laptop out, radio on. I flick between Radio One and Capital, then once I'm sick of hearing Ed Sheeran for the two hundredth time I switch it off and listen to the dripping tap instead. Don't get me wrong, I absolutely love Ed, but no song out there is so good that after a few hundred listens you wouldn't want to drive a power drill into your temple. Here's an interesting fact: like most people that live in Dover, I can't change radio stations without accidentally picking up French radio by mistake. You're probably thinking, 'Wow, Arron, how exotic! What undiscovered musical treats do you get to listen to on French radio?' I tell you what it is, mate. It's more bloody Ed Sheeran.

So I'm sat at my kitchen table and the power cord is running from here to where the kettle is normally connected. It's created a sort of limbo bar for the rest of the family to duck under whenever they come past, which at first the kids found hilarious. Now, however, after a few dozen trips and a couple of near decapitations the novelty has really started to wear off to be honest. On the table there's a half-drunk can of Diet Coke to the right of me and about seventeen empty cans to the left. Then the rest of the table is covered with wrappers from the few hundred Babybels I've eaten since I started today – which was only about an hour ago. Here is the biggest struggle I've faced while writing this book. By working mostly in the kitchen I've surrounded myself with food, which isn't good for a guy whose brain is constantly telling him to do anything other than write and whose stomach is yelling to his brain: why not get up and grab some food? You love food!

And what's even worse is that after eating all those Babybels, I'm now surrounded by red wax – which is a nightmare for anyone that likes to waste time as much as me, I tell you. I'm currently way less focused on the book and more focused on building a pretty sweet wax dinosaur. I'm so proud of my masterpiece that I've even taken a photo of it for the book. I wonder if it's worth calling up the publisher and asking if they'd be interested in doing another book with me, filled cover to cover with photos of all my various cheese wax dino creations. I'll email them later. Until then I'll just stick with this one: as you can see, rather than go for your more popular Tyrannosaurus Rex, I've opted for my personal favourite, the underrated Stegosaurus. The T-Rex is all about, you know, showy, you know what I mean? Now I hit a new problem. Staring at the little Stego, my brain's wandering again. I'm distracted by the little dude, and have decide not to write another single word until I find out what the plates on a Stegosaurus's back are for. Excuse me while I load up Google real quick. I'll be right back.

Okay, I'm back. Wow, that hour flew by. Turns out the plates were used mainly for protection, but also the Stegosaurus could pump blood into them to make them change colour to either ward off enemies or attract a mate. There you go, guys, I told you at the beginning this book would be educational, didn't I? By the way, I've left the kitchen and I'm in the lounge now. I also tried working upstairs on the bed, but there is literally no position you can get yourself into that doesn't result in you falling asleep instantly, or bending over so much you end up looking like the Hunchback of Notre-Dame. Grab your laptop and have a go yourself; just make sure that before you do you set your alarm for the morning. You have been warned.

So I'm in the lounge, and I've put the TV on for a bit of background noise. Just a bit of *I'm Alan Partridge* to help me concentrate and maybe inspire me a little b—

Oh dear. Well, that didn't work out too well. It's four hours later and I've blasted through both series. The laptop's not even been touched and the only reason I've snapped out of my *Partridge* coma is because Charlotte started having a go at me for leaving the kettle unplugged in the kitchen. I knew we should have had more plugs installed. You know what? I wonder how easy it is to install plugs yourself without bothering to pay for a bloke to come in? I'll just look it up on Google.

Jesus Christ, I've done it again. I started off looking for a how-to guide but somehow ended up looking at videos of alien conspiracy theories.

Okay, back to it, but I still need some noise in the background, so perhaps I should try putting on something I couldn't have less interest in. Fortunately *University Challenge* is on. There's no way I can get distracted by this. You could say I'm immune, I guess. Don't get me wrong, Jeremy Paxman's a bit of a lad, but the questions are so hard that it's impossible for me to come close to getting any correct. So what, the point in even tryi—

Wait, what time is it? Shit, here we go again! Another forty-five minutes wasted. I vaguely remember a question about flags which caught my interest, so I started looking up the origins of the Union Jack and before you know it, I'm browsing the internet desperately trying to find out whether or not there actually was a bloke called Jack who came up with the flag in the first place. Turns out no one actually knows why it's called Jack. Some people think it's because 'jack' used to mean small, so it literally meant a small flag, then other people think it has something to do with the '*jacke*ts' worn by the British. No, there is no bastard called Jack, so that was all a colossal waste of time. What the hell am I doing??? I'm supposed to be writing a book! Not letting myself get sent on wild goose chases by Jeremy bloody Paxman. But again, like I said before, at least we're all learning something, right? In fact I think you should start taking notes, there'll be a test at the end.

If there's one thing I've learned while writing this it's that working at home isn't that productive. I've written birthday cards with more words than I've managed today. Still, at least I've got a pretty awesome wax Stegosaurus to show for today's efforts. Tomorrow I'll work twice as hard, I promise.

Okay, today I'm out of the house. It's a massive cliché but I thought I'd give writing in a coffee shop a go. Have you ever gone to somewhere like Starbucks or Costa on a lunch break or on your way into work and wondered who the hell are these people that can afford to spend their days in a coffee shop when everyone else has to go to work? (Yes, yes, I know, Mr Facebook here is hardly one to talk). The answer is, those people are writers, and the coffee shop, my friend, is where writers go when they want to be seen writing something.

ME: 'What are you working on?'
HIPSTER STRANGER: 'A screenplay. You?'
ME: 'A book. How's your thing going?'
HIPSTER STRANGER: 'Not well, I've just spent my time looking at videos of animals lip-syncing to pop songs. How about yours?'
ME: 'Good, actually. Yesterday I researched the complete origins of the Union Jack.'
HIPSTER STRANGER: 'Oh great, good for you. So is it a history book?'
ME: 'No. Why, what would give you that impression?'

Of course that wasn't a real conversation. No chat like that would ever take place, because people writing in coffee shops do not acknowledge each other. If anything they're bitter rivals. To the hipster stranger I could be writing an even better movie script than the one he's writing. And for all I know, that hipster stranger could be writing his own Arron Crascall book. No, instead we keep our heads down and focus on our work, never exchanging so much as a 'y'alright?' with one another.

Right now, without looking away from my laptop, I can make out two writers in here with me; one bloke at roughly three o'clock opposite the paninis and toasties and another, older geezer at ten o'clock near the biscotti biscuits. The biscotti man has been here since I arrived. I got a good look at him as I queued for my grande skinny wet Americano (when in Rome). He looks every bit the coffee-shop writer: thick black hair with plenty of grey on the back and sides. He looks really focused in a pretty intense kind of way, and I can tell by the way he's holding his hand up to his mouth with his finger hooked over his lip that he's got to a particularly tricky bit. Although he's probably just having a really good sniff of his digit. He's wearing square black glasses, a dark blue woollen top and while I can't see anything below the table, my guess is he's wearing red chinos – he looks like one of those red trouser sort of blokes. He's not even blinking, he's so focused. When it comes to professional writers, this guy is the real deal. Well, he certainly *looks* the real deal; at the moment he's doing a lot more looking than writing, but then again, I also came to write and I'm just watching strangers instead.

Okay, what about the other guy? I think the panini man arrived soon after I sat down. I hadn't noticed him really, because it's only now, about twenty minutes later, that he's got out his laptop and started working. Without looking up I can tell he's younger than Biscotti; he has brown hair, a brown beard and a burgundy zip-up hoodie. Scruffy-looking. An amateur, and Biscotti knows it. TAP TAP TAPPY TAP! Biscotti's suddenly started tapping on his keyboard really hard. My guess is he wants Panini man to know he's the best writer in this joint. Panini doesn't respond, though. He just takes a sip of his drink and calmly gets on with his work. Biscotti man takes that as a victory and goes back to staring at the screen.

Then, TAPPY TAPPY TAPPY TAP! It's Panini man this time, whacking the keys with real determination. SHOTS FIRED! Biscotti is not impressed. It's like we're inside a saloon bar in some Western movie and Panini man just accidentally mugged off the baddest outlaw in town. Things are getting tense, and the whole of Starbucks knows it now. Biscotti tuts, shakes his head and makes his own loud keyboard noises. Then Panini goes louder, then Biscotti gets even louder still, then back and forth, both men tapping away louder and louder, convinced they are producing the best work. All eyes in Starbucks are now focused on the two blokes, who are furiously thrashing out letter after letter. Until the music suddenly cuts out in the shop and everything stops abruptly with a loud silence, all except the ludicrous, unnatural sound of two men finger-banging[11] their keyboards. Everyone stares. Biscotti and Panini look pretty embarrassed and awkwardly come to a stop. The whole coffee shop slowly returns to normal and both men return to their regular working volume. From where I'm sitting I can't tell if Panini man's fingers are bleeding or if it's just excess jam from his scone.

Well, that wasn't very helpful. While all that's gone on, I've made eff-all progress, because that's another habit of mine: people-watching. Wherever I am I'm fascinated by other people. If I'm standing on a busy train platform I study people and try and guess where they're going. In a restaurant I'm obsessed with what food other people order, and don't get me started on noticing arguments in public. It's like your very own live performance of *Jeremy Kyle* – they want you to watch, don't they? Sometimes I feel bad for not stepping in. And I probably shouldn't be booing them either.

And you can't sit there and judge me for people-watching, mate. Don't forget you're the one who's reading a book about someone else's life. Holding this book up to your face, you might as well be spying on me. That's just as bad as spying on people in public, yeah? No? Oh well, I guess you're right.

Okay, before we finish up this chapter, let's do a quick rundown of some of the other places I've tried to go to get work done.

---

11 Yeah, that's right, finger-banging. As in 'banging their keyboards with their fingers'. Why, what do you think finger-banging means? Pervert.

Places I've tried to work

The Train – you never know when inspiration will hit you, so don't be afraid to whip out your laptop on the train and start writing. You're better off doing that than waiting till you get home and potentially forgetting that zinger that's in your head. However, be prepared to have people looking over your shoulder while you type. And if you spot the person next to you raising a sly smile as they read, then that's great, but nothing can knock your confidence more than writing something you're proud of only for the lady next to you to roll her eyes and yawn. Well read this then, nosy: 'Arron deletes paragraph, puts laptop back in backpack and spends remaining journey fighting back tears. His feelings have well and truly been hurt by the lady in the lavender cardigan. Yes, that's right, I'm talking about you, lavender lady.'

The Park – I read somewhere online that chaining yourself to a machine does nothing for your creative juices. That you should get outside and be inspired by the real world. Try walking in the park recording talking notes into your phone, it said. I was also recommended an app that types up your words automatically, which sounds great for a lazy bastard like me, but it did warn that you might have to tweak the odd mistake. The odd mistake? It comes out making about as much sense as a drunk explaining to the police how he ended up with his trousers on top of a traffic light. To help you understand how bad it is, I've narrated the next paragraph into my phone, had it translated and made sure not to change a thing.

The Pub – Die writing in the pub. The people enshrined are a will camber destruction. Maid swore the pub Easter old main pub not a cruel trendy yum fur yum people. Phil fee to half a pint to but nothing more you woodland warrant to turn your Brookside intruder ramblings offer loan lee dunk sat on his owning the Korma.

The Toilet – Okay, now you're talking. As a father of three, the toilet has now become a real sanctuary to me. As you close the door and that lock turns, it can be the only time you ever find peace. Any other dads out there will agree with me. No one sobbing because they can't find one of the raccoons for their Sylvanian Families treehouse; no one begging you for Quavers or demanding you put *Paw Patrol* on the telly for the millionth time. This is your special place. A place of tranquillity, of quiet meditation and zen-like reflection. So what better time, then, to knock out another chapter of your book? I'll hold my hands up and say I reckon some of my best work has come when I've treated myself to a cheeky sit-down wee. Never a number two, though. Come on, mate, I'm not a monster. However, if you're thinking of doing this too, there is one important thing to bear in mind: is your laptop made of plastic or metal? If like me you have a metal one then you'll notice that when you first rest it on top of your naked legs it can be effin' freezing. Like someone has just subjected your lap to its very own ice bucket challenge. You can't dwell on it, though, because from this second you're on the clock. With every minute that ticks by and that laptop's switched on, it will slowly get hotter and hotter. You don't need a physics A-level to learn how easily metal conducts heat, and before you know it that machine that's perched only a few inches away from your sensitive bits will become hotter than a nuclear reactor. I guess in a way it's the perfect incentive you need to get that tricky chapter done in good time. Get carried away, though, and you'll have to spend the rest of your life explaining why the hair can't grow on the tops of your legs and why your laptop always stinks of bacon.

By the way, if you are thinking about writing your own book then my advice is to get out anywhere and do it. They say everyone has one book in them, so give it a go. Don't forget I'm the guy whose teacher once said, '*His writing lacks imagination and his spelling is weak*', so if I can write a book then anyone can. And even though right this second I'm sat at my laptop with a loud voice in the back of my head screaming, 'YOU'LL NEVER GET THIS FINISHED, ARRON SO YOU MIGHT AS WELL RELAX ON THE SOFA AND PLAY *BATTLEFIELD!*' the fact that you're reading this means that against all the odds I actually shut out my distractions long enough to get the thing done. So hopefully, guys, this chapter can offer you some amount of inspiration.

CHAPTER NINETEEN

TECHNOLOGY

This may come as a surprise to some people, but despite making a living off my mobile phone I'm actually terrible with technology. I can do everything I need when it comes to my videos; filming them, editing them and getting them uploaded to my socials, but ask me to do anything else and I'm useless. Even something as simple as setting the alarm on my phone has me scratching my head.

Let's start with the phone because that's got to be the most important piece of tech we all own. And if you think about what phones were like fifteen years ago, how they've changed is pretty ridiculous. I bet most young people today walk past a Carphone Warehouse in the high street and think to themselves, 'What's a carphone?' In my day it was the most luxurious thing you could own – if someone's dad had a carphone, you'd bet they'd be boasting about it in the playground. It was the most mobile a phone could get at the time, even though it looked like a massive brick attached to a briefcase and was so heavy it had to be driven around in the back seat of the car. That, my young friends, is a carphone; and if you want one I suggest you check out eBay because I doubt you'll see Apple announcing one any time soon.

Speaking of young people, I find it incredible how good most kids are with smartphones. Before my Alfie and Mia even turned two they were swiping, pinching and moving between apps with the same speed as Tom Cruise in *Minority Report*. It's intimidating – especially for someone as useless as me. And there are few things more embarrassing than asking your four-year-old to set that morning alarm for you. I wonder if this is a growing trend. Where do you reckon we'll be in fifty years' time? I reckon babies will come out of the womb knowing how to get three stars in every level of *Angry Birds*.

Despite handing over hundreds of pounds' worth of phone to my children, my phone has never been mistreated enough to get one of those trendy 'smashed screen' looks other people love so much. Smashed screens are as much of a fashion statement in the noughties as ripped jeans were in the '90s. It makes me laugh when I look over and see someone trying to watch a film on their phone even though it's busted into a thousand pieces. It turns out *Fast & Furious 8* doesn't get any better when it looks like you're watching it through a kaleidoscope. Especially when every time The Rock comes on screen it looks like he was drawn by Pablo Picasso.

It's surprising that my screen has never been smashed, especially when you consider the number of times I've been so frustrated with my phone that I've wanted to throw it against the nearest wall. There are hundreds of things technology does that really piss me off, but here's a rundown of my top eight.

8. Autocorrect.

Okay, this is nothing new but it doesn't make it any less infuriating. Thanks to autocorrect, some words are now just part of the modern language; like ducking. If I tell you I'm having a ducking bad day, you know exactly what I mean. It's also annoying how you write a word one way and that automatically becomes the default spelling. Like years ago

I wrote 'really' in all capitals on my phone so now whenever I write that word again it comes out in all caps, which makes everything I write sound sarcastic. Sentences like: 'I'm REALLY looking forward to seeing you this weekend', 'I REALLY like your outfit today' and 'I'm REALLY sorry I lost your number.'

7. Terms & Conditions.

Has anyone, in the history of the world, ever actually read the terms and conditions to anything? Apple seem to update their T&Cs every couple of months and I, like everyone else out there, just click 'accept' like an obedient puppy doing whatever his master tells him to do. Has anyone at *Apple* even read them? And what do you think is written there? I reckon somewhere out there right now is a lawyer at Apple writing the next Terms and Conditions. He's hunched over in a dark office cubicle typing away and crying to himself because he's going to do all this hard work and no one will even bother with the first paragraph.

6. Pocket dialling.

Years of innovation and still phones can't tell the difference between my thumb and my house keys. Apologies to anyone who I've ever pocket-dialled, and if I have pocket-dialled you and all you heard was passionate heavy breathing, don't get too excited, it was probably just me trying to climb a hill. No passion there. Unless there was a Burger King at the top. By the way, some people call this phenomenon 'bum dialling', which brings a whole new meaning to 'cracking your screen'.

5. Earphone yanking.

When you're listening to music on the phone and get your earphones caught on something like a door handle. There is no pain greater in this world than the feeling of having your earphones pulled out of your head when you're not expecting it. One second you're bowling along all cool with some AC/DC playing into your lugs, then BANG! Your head is thrown back and you look like a bull that's just had its head lassoed by some redneck at a rodeo. It's impossible to style this one out.

NB: Take care when needing to fart if you've got head-phones on. Make sure you have a really good look around you because while you've got that music playing, it's abso-lutely impossible to gauge how loud it's going to be.

4. Earphone entanglement.
Sticking with earphones; when you go to listen to music but the damn things are coiled up like a cluster of Pot Noodle you dropped on the floor last night. You'll have a crack at uncoiling them, but after half an hour you've only made it worse, so give up. Looks like you'll be listening to that couple on the bus arguing behind you after all.

3. Lying batteries.
When your phone dies but it didn't even reach 0 per cent. If I'd known the battery was going to shut down at 20 per cent, I wouldn't have wasted the last half an hour taking a few thousand pictures of me as a dog on Snapchat.

2. Cable erosion.
Why do all phone chargers end up frayed and full of exposed wires? You know you risk electrocuting yourself every time you plug it in but you're happy with that – there's no way you're spending thirty quid on a new lead.

1. Vibration hunting.
Losing your phone when it's on silent. This happens to me on a daily basis, and yet I still refuse to take it off silent. There's nothing more frustrating than having to hunt down a phone when it's ringing and all you can hear is that vibrate sound. Seriously, you go into every room looking for it and

that noise carries. Wherever you are the damn thing sounds like it's right next to you. It's taunting you. You think you're better than me, do you? You enjoy hiding like this, do you? Let's see you laughing when I throw you against the . . . found it! Yeah, it was under the sofa cushion all along.

The phone has become an extension of our own bodies. We're so used to it being near us at all times that whenever you reach into your pocket and realise it's not there, there's a massive fear that runs through your entire body. And it's such a huge disappointment when you sit on the toilet, rummage into your trouser pocket and find nothing but a couple of receipts and that Freddo bar you forgot you had. Oh well, it could be worse; at least you have those receipts to read. Listen carefully; if you ever find yourself in this exact situation, please learn from my mistakes and resist the temptation to eat that melted Freddo. You'll find that leaving a public toilet with melted chocolate all over your fingers and lips is incredibly difficult to explain.

The greatest mobile phone of all time was of course the Nokia 3310. In the early noughties, if you didn't have one of those you could pretty much kiss your social life goodbye. You want great games? It had *Snake* – the greatest phone game ever created. You want instant messaging? Forget WhatsApp, with nine buttons and predictive text, you could communicate faster writing an SMS on here than on any of today's phones. And what's more, it could store TEN WHOLE MESSAGES on that SIM card! You want to be able to express yourself with a new background? Don't waste your time cycling through your Camera Roll, get yourself down to the market and buy an overpriced replacement cover! Nothing says *you* like a sweet tiger-print case. Want to browse the worldwide web on the go? Screw 4G – with the upgraded 3330, you could book those cinema tickets from the comfort of any park bench with WAP (did anyone actually use WAP? I still don't really know what it means). And finally, the thing that proves the 3310 was years ahead of its successors, Nokia thought the phone would be better off being built without a headphone jack more than a decade before Apple decided the iPhone didn't need one. And finally, let's talk battery life: the phone could run for weeks before you needed to charge it. These days people have to carry around power bricks and spare phone chargers just to make it through the day.

Seriously, though, the 3310 was a special device, and was firmly by my side throughout my late teens. It truly has earnt its place alongside the likes of the wheel, the aeroplane and the SodaStream as one of the greatest inventions of all time.

Like I said, I am useless with technology, but you could be the biggest tech whizz in the world and you'd still fall into some of the same old traps that everyone else does. Especially when it comes to social media. Who out there hasn't lost hours falling down a rabbit hole innocently going through someone's wall on Facebook? You're just scrolling along, laughing at the odd hilarious status update, flicking through a few classic photos then BAM! Your finger slips and you accidentally tap the like button. It's very difficult to explain to people why you're liking a bikini snap of an ex-girlfriend that was uploaded back in 2007. You've gone so far back in their timeline that it's amongst a load of status updates where people started them all by writing 'is'. As in 'Arron IS awake at midnight drunkenly swiping through his ex's holiday albums.'

The biggest trap, though, is Instagram. What sick monster thought it was a good idea to make double-tap the shortcut to liking a picture? Now I know I'm coming across like I spend all my time perving over people's pictures on social media – I promise, mate, I don't – but how many times have you double-tapped a picture thinking it will zoom in and give you a closer look but ended up liking it by mistake? Well, you can blame the evil bastards at Instagram for that one.

Okay, let me tell you a little story about my biggest-ever tech-based cock-up. It happened a few years ago and landed me in a lot of trouble with one of the largest tech companies in the world. At the time it gave me a lot of sleepless nights, not to mention a fair amount of ribbing from some of my followers online. These days, though, I can look back on it and laugh because it was an absolute rookie mistake.

Before I get into it, first I need to pull back the curtain a little bit and talk about what I do for a living. Making videos is my full-time job – and that doesn't mean I spend ten minutes a day making a video, then the rest of it sitting on my bum playing *Call of Duty*. They take time to film, they take time to edit and they take a really long time just to come up with the idea in the first place (which, fair enough, may often come to me when I'm on my bum playing *Call of Duty*). So as this is a full-time job, I need to make money from it so that I can pay my mortgage and buy food for the family (and purchase the latest map packs for *Call of Duty*). The simplest way for that to happen is by doing a sponsored video. It's nothing shady, and no, it doesn't make me a sell-out, thank you very much. My entire livelihood is based on my reputation for making content that people find entertaining. You're only as good as your last video, which is why I make sure that everything I upload, whether or not it's sponsored, is something I know my followers will enjoy. Besides, anything that is an ad says AD right the under the video, so you'll always know if I'm attempting to brainwash you for some corporate G-man.

Now, this story involves two massive tech companies, neither of which I'm allowed to mention by name for legal reasons, so rather than call them by their actual names, for the purposes of this story

I'm going to call one of the companies 'Ant' and the other company 'Dec'. Simple? Of course not, but there's no other way.

Okay, a couple of years ago 'Ant' called me up and asked me to do a series of three sponsored videos for them. 'Ant' produce loads of different tech products, including a popular range of mobile phones. On this occasion it was 'Ant's' latest phone handset that they wanted me to promote, and it was difficult to say no to; not just because 'Ant' was such a big company but also because I had some really good ideas for videos that I knew would be well received online. The only slightly awkward thing is that I've been using a 'Dec' phone for years, and it was written pretty explicitly in my contract with 'Ant' that as long as I was doing these three videos, I could only be seen using an 'Ant' phone. But like any normal person, I thought, 'You know what? That's an incredibly small sacrifice to make when you're getting paid to film some stupid sketches', so I agreed to the terms.

I was really happy with the first video; it was a good joke without obviously being an ad and was well received both by people online and by the guys at 'Ant'. Then I recorded the second video and I thought that turned out even better; I uploaded it the same night it was shot and went to bed feeling confident that the way things were going, the third video was going to be fantastic. How wrong I was.

Probably about five minutes after uploading that second video, my phone was buzzing. My head was already on the pillow, which means there was no way I was answering that call, so I turned to face the other way and let the phone ring out. But the bloody thing just buzzed again. And again. And again. I'm actually the sort of person that can sleep quite easily through things like vibrating phones, but I was receiving subtle messages from Char that I should probably pick this one up (she was kicking me in the shins over and over again). I picked up the phone and on the other end was my agent. 'What the hell have you done, Arron?' he barked down the line. What had I done? I thought. My brain scrambled, and all I could think of was that I'd had a late-night binge on Coco Pops and left the bowl out in the lounge without washing it up, but I couldn't think why this would concern my agent. 'You've got to pull the "Ant" video right now, Arron. Delete it quick.'

In a frenzy I ended the call and loaded up Facebook. As soon as I took the phone away from my ear I knew exactly what I'd done. It was right there in my hand. I was holding the same phone I had used ten minutes ago to upload the video. The same video I'd been using for years. My 'Dec' phone. Uh-oh.

When Facebook opened, I could see it. It was exactly what I feared. There, below the video, amongst an onslaught of abuse from some friendly (and not-so-friendly) followers were three little words: 'Uploaded via "Dec" phone.' Ah. Not exactly what you want to see underneath a sponsored video for 'Ant' phones. I deleted the video as soon as I could and after a night of very little sleep I received the news that 'Ant' were pulling the plug on the deal. Turns out they were pretty sensitive about the whole 'Dec' thing, and sadly for me I was getting a ton of abuse online, and even more importantly, no deal meant those new *Call of Duty* map packs weren't getting purchased any time soon.

I'm so bad at technology that you could give me a tin opener and I'd lock myself out of it. So every time a new piece of technology comes out, I'm always terrified about what sort of damage I'm going to do. Like, the latest tech craze these days are 'smart homes'. Does that phrase mean anything to you? If not, basically what it means is that thanks to various fancy devices, you can control all manner of things around the house with just your voice. It's like Siri for your home. You walk around talking out loud, asking questions and issuing demands; things like, 'Turn the lights off in the living room' or 'Add cornflakes to my shopping list' and 'How is the traffic today?' If you ask me, it's fine but it's not realistic. These are the sorts of questions you should be able to ask:

Do I look a bit mooby in this top?

Can you let me know thirty seconds before Char gets back so I can look busy when she walks in?

Can you entertain the kids while I go back to bed instead?

I said can you entertain the kids while I go back to bed?

No, not back to bread, back to BED. What does 'back to bread' even mean?

No, you know what, it doesn't matter, are you okay just babysitting the kids for a bit?

The KIDS! Can you babysit the KIDS!? If I meant fridge I would have asked you to babysit the fridge, wouldn't I?

NO, I DON'T WANT BABYBELS FROM THE FRIDGE!

Actually, since you're offering . . .

I don't mean to sound melodramatic, but have the people making these things never seen *The Terminator*? Everyone knows that one day technology will become too intelligent for us and will wage war on humankind. So what are we doing making tech smarter and giving it control over our homes and every other aspect of our day-to-day lives? We're walking into a death trap here, people! Again, I know this is coming off as a bit doom and gloom, but if you wake up one morning and the T-1000 is knocking at your door trying to harvest your organs, then don't blame me.

Join the resistance today, people. Put down your phones! Rip off your Fitbits! Throw your laptop out of the window! Because today we begin our fightback against technology! Let's make our stand right now, so that future generations won't know the struggle that awaits them in the future. So that they will never live in fear. So that they won't have to spend every waking hour on the run from the robot armies of Cyberdyne Systems. Stand tall with me brothers and sisters, and let's fight evil technology together!

Having said all that, I do like Google Maps, so let's just see how we get on for now, shall we? Besides, there is one thing in particular technology has given us that I am grateful for every single day. Something I'll never be able to give up. Something very dear to my heart, and by a massive distance the longest relationship I've ever had . . .

CHAPTER TWENTY

VIDEO GAMES

Sega.

How do you pronounce that word? This is an important test, so I'll give you another go.

Sega.

If you look at it and are not instantly hearing 'Say-gah!', the melodic, robotic way your Megadrive would sing every time you boot up *Sonic the Hedgehog*, then I'm sorry, mate, we simply cannot be friends.

You see, never mind our future war against the machines; right now there is a more urgent, bloody war raging between hardcore gamers such as myself and a group of lousy, no-good, bunch of impostors who, just because they open up *Candy Crush Saga* for five minutes during their morning commute, claim to be gamers too. I'm sorry, but unless you can tell me your KDR (Kill Death Ratio) on *Battlefield* to the nearest three decimal places, then would you kindly piss off and come back to me when you know what you're talking about?

I'm not saying that the only games you can play are shooters, either; I'm just saying there's a massive difference between the dedication needed to accomplish something in the sort of games I play and the sort of games they play. Those part-timers, who rock back and forth on the train, tapping away on their phone simply as an excuse not to look up and acknowledge the person in front of them, will never understand the plight of a proper gamer. They won't know the feeling of waking up early on a Saturday to receive a new game in the post, loading it up straight away, playing it for a bit, then looking down at your watch to realise it's four o'clock on the Monday morning, you've not slept or washed for two days, you stink of pizza and Fanta and you're due at work in a few hours' time. That's a gamer.

Now people might hear that, shake their head and judge me for wasting my time, but my fellow gamers will understand that that two-day binge would have included some incredible entertainment you just can't get in books, or in films. When I play games, I'm often hooked either by a compelling story as I'm swept away on an epic journey, or a compelling sense of accomplishment as I level up my character, or a compelling sense of bloodlust pwning noob after noob with tasty headshots.[12]

Some people say video games are bad for you. Well they're not, mate. It's escapism, just like any movie or book out there. Playing *Mortal Kombat* as a kid, I punched a dude's head clean off his shoulders, cut someone in half with my hat and ripped a guy's heart out of his chest with my bare hands, and I haven't tried any of them in real life (granted, I don't think any of them are actually possible in real life). If violent games cause violent behaviour, then why don't non-violent games cause non-violent behaviour? Why when you look out the window do you never see Italian plumbers eating mushrooms, jumping on turtles and headbutting floating blocks of bricks? Exactly. Although fair play, Mario, if I was knocking back as many magic mushrooms as you, I wouldn't be leaping

12 If these words mean nothing to you, scroll down for a handy gaming glossary.

about rescuing princesses, I'd be sitting in my shower in tears, too scared to leave the bathroom.

Glossary of gaming terms

Before we go any further, I think it's important you understand some really important phrases that all proper gamers use.

Camping – used when playing shooters. It means taking a position that allows you to easily pick off opponents like fish in a barrel while you remain almost invisible inside a bush. Is camping an elite strategy or a cheap, noobish trick? Your answer to that question depends on what side of the gun barrel you're on.

Noob – short for newbie, this is someone who is inexperienced with the game, and a pretty standard insult to throw at someone you've just pwned.

Pwned – utterly dominating someone in a competitive game. It's pronounced like 'owned' but with a p at the beginning. Who knows why the p is in there? Gamers are just crap at spelling, I guess.

Teabag – after pwning someone, it's only customary to perform a teabag on them. This involves getting your character to crouch and stand and crouch and stand over and over to simulate their virtual testicles bobbing up and down on the face of your opponent's dead body. You have to agree it's pretty classy.

Rage quit – 'pulling the plug' on an online game because you've been sent into an angry frenzy by your opponent.

Maybe it's because you've lost your tenth game in a row, but it's more likely because they're teabagging you again.

Lag – a delay in the game caused by poor internet connection that puts the player at a severe disadvantage. It's the number one excuse for rage-quitting noobs that can't handle being pwned, let alone another teabagging from my virtual testes.

Far from being a bad influence, you can actually learn a lot playing video games. Obviously there are loads of boring educational ones that are specifically designed to help you learn. Then there's management sims like *Football Manager* and *Rollercoaster Tycoon* that can help you understand what it's like to manage a football team or a theme park. Simulators are actually so realistic that you can perform a twelve-hour flight from London to Los Angeles, with access to all the same controls a real pilot has, right there on your computer. Although it's just a sim, so rather than touching down amongst the hot sandy beaches and blazing Californian sun, as soon as you step out of this cockpit you're still in your grotty bedroom with the curtains drawn and ten missed calls from the fancy-dress shop demanding to know when you're going to return that pilot's uniform.

Some games are extra special because they teach you things without you even realising it. Have you ever seen someone play *Assassin's Creed*? It's basically a history lesson disguised as a video game. It's the one that sees you play this old-timey assassin that spends most of his time climbing up some of Europe's famous landmarks. Places like the Pantheon in Rome, St Mark's in Venice and Notre-Dame in Paris. I've never seen these places in real life, and yet after the days I've spent climbing them in the game I not only know their names, I also know every detail of them, brick by brick. In fact I probably know more about St Paul's Cathedral than I do about my own house. This sort of knowledge stays with you because you've not just read it in a book; you've actually done it. And after a couple of days with *Assassin's Creed*, you won't be able to walk past an old building without working out exactly how you would climb it.

Speaking of history, thanks to shooters like *Call of Duty* and *Battlefield* I now have the kind of intimate knowledge of World War II that would put Winston Churchill to shame. 'When did the Russians win back Stalingrad from the Germans?' Nineteen forty three mate, easy. 'How many allies landed on the beaches in Normandy on D-Day?' One hundred and fifty thousand – come on that was the first level. 'When was the Bay of Pigs?' Don't try and catch me out, that's not even World War II. But since you ask, it was 1961. Honestly, I've completed *Black Ops* about twenty times, so you've really got to try harder.

Also in terms of skills learned, while I'm pretty confident I'll never fight in a proper war, thanks to my extensive military training in these games I reckon I could give some of that army lot a run for their money. So long as someone told me what the reload button was and made sure the look controls weren't inverted, I'd be unstoppable. Oh, and better turn friendly fire off just to be sure. I hear there's no hardcore mode IRL.

In fact, if what many people have predicted does comes true, and zombies rise from their graves and terrorise the world with an unstoppable craving for human flesh, I'm 99 per cent sure that the only people left standing would be the hardcore gaming community. We're the only ones equipped to handle this sort of shit. Whether using a rifle, a grenade or a frying pan, fending off the undead is second nature to us lot. As long as you remember that there are no respawns. Well, actually, I guess as you'll turn into a zombie yourself then there will be one respawn at least.

Gaming is an emotional pastime to say the least. It's full of outrageous highs and lows. Here's a rundown of some of those moments every gamer has experienced in their lifetime and that the uninitiated out there simply will never understand.

LOW!

Having that mate who finds it hilarious to keep pausing the game repeatedly. Every time you unpause it, they pause it again. It wasn't funny the first time, and it definitely isn't funny the two hundredth time.

HIGH!

Finding a new camping spot that nobody knows about.

LOW!

Getting teabagged by a little **** after someone discovers your new camping spot.

HIGH!

Hitting that guy in the moving car with a headshot from the other side of the map.

LOW!

Being that guy in the moving car getting hit with a headshot from the other side of the map.

HIGH!

Completing an objective when you're the last person in the team alive and the rest are forced to spectate and witness your epic solo skills.

LOW!

Being asked to pause an online game. When will she learn it simply cannot be done???

HIGH!

Scoring a screamer from outside the box in *FIFA*.

LOW!

Realising you've been shooting with long balls all match because someone set the controller to *Pro Evo* controls.

HIGH!

Hitting your mate with a well-placed green shell just before the finish line to steal the win on *Mario Kart*.

LOW!

Having the mates round to play *Mario Kart* but realising you don't have enough controllers to go round.

HIGH!

Hearing your Xbox make that pop noise as you unlock a new achievement. You sat there for ages pressing the A button over and over to complete that 'jump a million times' challenge and now you feel like a real champion.

LOW!

Coming to terms with the fact that the eight hours it took to get that achievement might not have been the most productive use of your time.

HIGH!

Getting your first job so you can finally afford all the video games you want.

LOW!

Getting your first job and not having the time to play any video games at all.

HIGH!

Playing online for the first time and discovering there are more ladies on there than you thought there'd be.

LOW!

Realising all those 'ladies' are high-pitched prepubescent boys.

VERY LOW!

Explaining to yourself how you just got your arse handed to you by said bunch of prepubescent boys.

Gaming is all about competition, and the most fierce competition doesn't take place on virtual racetracks or gang hideouts, it takes place on internet forums, with angry gamers arguing with each other about what games are the best. Understanding the various factions within the gaming community is a lot like understanding the various factions within an American high school. You've got to be in it to really understand it, and just like an American high school, getting into it is very difficult once you're over thirty.

The most brutal debates are the console wars. Xbox owners hate PlayStation owners, PlayStation owners hate Xbox owners, Nintendo owners hate both but they don't really hate Nintendo owners because they don't really see them as a threat. Then they all hate PC gamers, and PC gamers hate all of them. Still with me?

Then beyond that you have inverted vs non-inverted, which is like asking does up mean up or does up mean down? Which is of course stupid, because everyone knows up means up so stop plaguing my settings with inverted controls you idiot. And there's loads more, too: single player vs multiplayer, online vs offline, handheld console vs home console, control stick vs D-pad, game-play vs graphics, resolution vs frame rate, Ryu vs Ken, Mario vs Sonic, *Pro Evo* vs *FIFA*, Ultimate team vs be a pro, *Forza* vs *Gran Turismo*, *Dota* vs *League*, *Call of Duty* vs *Battlefield* and so on and so on. It's a civil war as bloody as any other one in history.

But nothing divides the gaming community more than one phenomenon in particular. There is a single game that, depending on who you ask, is either the pinnacle of all entertainment or the biggest piece of trash you'll ever see on a screen. I am of course talking about the one and only *Minecraft*.

We have to ask, is *Minecraft* even a game? There's no right or wrong answer to that question except there totally is, and no it's totally not. Calling yourself a gamer when all you play is *Mine-craft* is like saying you love movies but all you watch is *You've*

Been Framed. I love *You've Been Framed*, but it's not a movie, is it? Exactly. *Minecraft* is a drug and the world's children are hooked on it. Think about it, there's no story, there's no real sense of competition, it looks hideous, and yet everyone under the age of twenty seems to dedicate every waking hour to it. Load up YouTube and you'll notice that these days it's 50 per cent cat videos and 50 per cent *Minecraft* tutorials. If they had made the main character in *Minecraft* a cat then I swear they would have claimed total domination of the internet.

For anyone who doesn't know what *Minecraft* is, then the simplest thing to do is look in the general direction of a child, any child, because they're all playing it, all the time: at home, in parks, on the bus, outside of school on street corners (like I said, this thing is a drug). When you load up the game, the first thing you notice is that it looks like complete and utter gash. Everything is made up of ugly blocks. That house? A block. That door? A block. That bed? A block. That sheep? A white block. That pig? A pink block. Your character? A block with a face. Not only is it ugly, it's pointless. The aim of the game is there is no aim. You beat up a tree (yes, you beat up a tree) to make a wood. You beat up another tree to make another wood. You join the woods together to make a stick which makes the next few dozen trees easier to beat up. Then you beat up some mountains to make some rocks, then you dedicate your next couple of lifetimes repeating this process until you have enough woods and rocks to build an ugly house that you hate because you're not entirely happy with where you put one of the downstairs windows, and you know that in order to change it you'd have to beat up the entire house and start again.

You know what? Confession time here, people. I do actually think *Minecraft* is pretty great (Arron, you hypocrite!). It is an impressive toolbox that lets everyone create whatever they want, limited only by their imagination (and the fact that whatever you build will still just be a bunch of blocks). Little Alfie is so obsessed with *Minecraft*, it reminds me of the obsession I had growing up with Lego. And that's what it is – it's Lego. It's a toy. And when all is said and done, you wouldn't call Lego a video game, would you? Well, unless you count *Lego: Batman*, *Lego: Star Wars*, *Lego: Indiana Jones*, *Lego: Marvel*, *Lego: Jurassic Park*, *Lego: Lord of the Rings*, *Lego: Harry Potter* and *Lego: Dimensions*, but why would you be like that?

My top ten video games of all time

10. *Street Fighter 2*
9. *Streets of Rage 2*
8. *The Legend of Zelda: Ocarina of Time*
7. *Burnout Paradise*
6. *Mario Kart 8*
5. *GoldenEye*
4. *Super Mario 64*
3. *Call of Duty: Black Ops*
2. *Call of Duty: Modern Warfare 2*
1. *Battlefield 1*

The last thing I want to bring up, guys, is the word 'geek'. Listen, I'm a geek and I'm very proud of it, but these days I feel the term has changed. It doesn't mean what it did back in my day – for better and worse. When I was young I was a geek because I spent my days locked in my room reading comics, watching wrestling and playing video games. These days, thanks to the success of shows like *Big Bang Theory* and movies like *X-Men* and *Iron Man*, it's now considered cool to be a geek. What the hell? If I could go back in time to tell twelve-year-old Arron that when he grew up he'd be proud of being a geek, he would have told me to get lost

– although that's probably because I would have just interrupted his game of *Mortal Kombat* (miraculous vision from the future or not, there's no interrupting young Crascall once he's midway through a game).

I'm really happy that this special pastime that has been important to me since I was tiny is now being accepted by the masses, but to me it still all feels a bit fake. Online you get 'so-called gamers' posing proudly with their PS4s when it doesn't take a genius to point out that they're actually holding an Xbox controller. Or the ironic T-shirts with superheroes on them (as if you've ever read a *Batman* comic in your life, mate). The absolute worst, though, is the people who think it's fashionable to walk around wearing glasses with no lenses in them. How insensitive is that? Poor eyesight is a physical deficiency. The only thing more offensive would be for those people to go out and get their own guide dog just because they like the way they go with their trainers. People with lensless glasses have no appreciation for the daily struggle our geek community have had to endure wearing their thick, plasticky specs: the name-calling, the endless bog washes, the atomic wedgies. I'm not saying no one is allowed to wear glasses. Just that until you know what it's like to have your underwear pulled out from your trousers, high into the air and over your head, then I'm sorry, you don't get to wear them, mate. And you most definitely don't get to call yourself a geek.

CHAPTER TWENTY-ONE

THE IN/OUT DEBATE

No, don't worry, this isn't going to be me banging on about Brexit for an entire chapter. This is about a dilemma that's gone on much longer than some tired decision about Europe. It's perhaps the oldest question our species has ever faced. A question that has troubled us humans since the years of the cavemen: do we go out tonight? Or do we just stay in, snuggle up on the boar skin, watch some cave drawings and eat whatever's left of that pig carcass from last night?

There are two types of person in this world: the type that spends their days constantly coming up with excuses to avoid going out at night, and the type of person that looks for any excuse they can to get out of the house.

I've spent a great deal of my life in both camps, and if you ask me, whether you'd rather go out or stay in has a lot to do with how old you are. Your feelings change gradually as you get older. For instance, when you're young and you're old enough to drink (or old-looking enough to get served), then you find yourself obsessed with getting out as often as you can. The choice between going out to the pub on a Friday night or spending it at home with Mum and Dad is as easy a question to answer as, 'Would you like fries with that?'

When you're young, you are only limited by how much money you have (what sixteen-year-old has enough money to go out every night?) and more importantly, how likely you are to get served. Growing up, I was afflicted with something all teenagers dread: No Beard Syndrome, which is a condition brutal enough to completely destroy any underage drinker's chances of getting served at the bar. For some reason, as soon as every young man turns fifteen, they either continue having the same smooth cheeks they've had since they were a baby (save for a few outbreaks of volcanic acne), or overnight they sprout huge amounts of hair and transform into full-on werewolves. Fortunately there were enough 'werewolves' in our group at college that if the fresh-cheeked amongst us kept a low profile and didn't cause too much trouble, then you could get away with drinking all night without being chucked out.

Pubs were one thing, but the real test was always getting into a nightclub. Dover's never been known for its clubs, but for those nights when we'd venture to Deal or Folkstone for a taste of the nightclub scene, we were really running the gauntlet. Who out there hasn't experienced the terror of sitting in the queue outside a club hoping they'll turn a blind eye to the fact that you obviously look like a child? Especially when the only ID you're packing is your battered old Sewing Machine Licence.

Unlike in the movies, our school didn't have some racket that was handing out fake IDs to everyone. In my day you just had to hide behind a werewolf, keep your head down and put on your best 'grown-up voice'. Did you ever have it too, when, even as you were walking down the road towards the club, you'd try and peel off away from the youngest-looking in the group and make sure you were next to the one with the biggest moustache? With any luck, once you reached the door the bouncer would take pity on you and just let you in. And can you remember the relief you felt when you got into a club when you were underage? It was like you'd just got all six balls and the bonus ball in the lottery. You'd be over the moon – until you had to pay to get in. It'd be ten quid at least, which would always be enough to guarantee that for the rest of the night you'd be drinking one VK Ice and a lot of tap water.

It was also here, in the foyer of the nightclub, that most people faced their greatest dilemma: if someone didn't get in, would you all leave to stay as a unit or would you write them off as collateral damage and ditch them? I'm ashamed to say we did on occasion ditch the odd person that didn't get in, but to be fair, the majority of the time *I* was the one getting ditched!

That's what it was like for me growing up. And as the dating scene was heating up, it was all about going out to keep them interested. But as you get older, and you start to settle down with someone, the urge to go out starts to diminish. It's like deep down our instinct kicks in and says, 'You've got yourself a mate, your work is done, now just stay in and watch *Take Me Out* instead.'

Many a night during our relationship Char and I have asked ourselves the same in/out question, and we've almost always come to the same conclusion:

'*Shall we go out and hit the bars for a drink?*'
'*We could. But if we stayed in then for the price of one glass of wine, we could get a whole bottle.*'
'*Shall we go out and watch a film?*'
'*We could, but what's the point in buying a massive telly if we're just going to go somewhere else to watch a film? Besides, our sofa is much comfier.*'
'*Shall we go out and have a nice romantic meal?*'
'*Put your coat down, babe, I've already ordered us a Chinese.*'

I firmly believe that deep down, everyone wants to stay at home, really. A lot of going out is just peer pressure, and deciding whether or not to go out is about either giving in to peer pressure or giving in to your overwhelming laziness. If you want proof that people naturally prefer to stay at home, next time someone at work asks you what you're doing this weekend, tell them you're doing absolutely nothing and watch their faces drop with jealousy.

Foolproof(ish) excuses for avoiding a night out

'I'm on babysitting duty tonight.' (Hard to pull off if you don't have a kid, but try it anyway.)

'I'm here right now. Can you not see me? We've already chatted tonight. Rude.'

'I think I'm allergic to moonlight.'

'I'm bleeding from my anus.' (They never ask questions after that.)

'My dog just ate a grape and I'm pretty sure it's poisonous . . . Yes that's right, I have a dog now . . . sure, his name? It's err . . . Paddy? Yes, Paddy . . . what breed? Err . . . brown? . . . You know what, I don't think you'll be able to meet her – I mean him – yeah, sadly it looks like the poison is already taking effect. Yep, yeah, he's gone.'

Staying in has its fair share of dilemmas, though. The main one being deciding what to watch on TV. These days with the invention of On Demand telly, we have practically every TV show and movie ever made at our fingertips, and yet it is impossible for any couple to agree on something they both want to watch. You can watch something *you* want to watch, and the other half will agree but really spend the whole time on their phone. Or you can watch something *they* want to watch and you'll be the one on your phone instead. There's no such thing as something you both want to watch. The alternative is, of course, you both compromise on something and neither of you really want to watch it so you both end up spending the whole time on your phones. But you'd both much rather be on the sofa sat on your phone than out in that bar looking at your phone because the music's too loud to have a conversation. (Wow, I sound like such an old man!)

Something happens when you get older. A life event that almost instantly turns the whole in/out debate on its head. I'm talking about the day you have kids. Almost as soon as that baby bursts out from your missus you go from, 'Let's just veg out on the sofa tonight', to 'OH MY GOD GET ME OUTSIDE PLEASE, I'M BEGGING YOU, I'M TRAPPED.' Okay, okay I'm exaggerating, of course having kids is amazing and brilliant and wonderful and some of the most fun you could possibly have, but once they're around, you look forward to the two or three nights a year you and your other half can go out like it's Christmas. I know what you're thinking: 'Why don't you stop complaining, Arron, and just get a babysitter?' Well let me tell you, babysitting has become ridiculous now. I remember when Amy did a bit of babysitting she'd get paid ten, maybe fifteen quid for a night's work, which wasn't bad considering she just had to sit on her bum and watch TV for a few hours. These days, though, if you want a babysitter you're looking at at least fifty quid! I might try and open up a pub with a crèche built in – that way you'd get loads of parents turning up dropping off their kids and getting wasted. Then I guess you'd end up in a tricky position where your three-year-old then became your designated driver. Oh well, they have to learn to drive sometime.

As well as the age thing, you have to remember that going out means very different things to men than it does to women. For most men, going out is just a matter of location. To us what we're doing is exactly the same, we're just drinking 'there' instead of 'here'. For many women, however, going out is an event; it requires days to prepare for, and on the night they'll need at least a couple of hours to get themselves ready. Meanwhile, men need just enough time to spray on some deodorant and put on a shirt. No one can explain why we're so different. I'm sure if you opened up Stephen Hawking's book he'd probably have a chapter explaining that it's because when women step into the bathroom, rather than using the door like the rest of us, they step in through a wormhole and exist in a totally different, parallel dimension where time moves a thousand times slower than our own. That, or because women just have much higher standards than us filthy blokes.

This in/out debate is one of many everyday stresses that might not seem like a big deal on its own, but combined with other little pressures, it's no wonder we've all become such a grumpy bunch over the years. What we need to do is unwind and relax, which is exactly the point of our next chapter.

CHAPTER TWENTY-TWO

MINDFULNESS

I hope by now you've learned a lot about me. That's probably the main job of a book about me, right? But I want you to learn a thing or two about yourself, too. Before you start freaking out, no, I haven't hacked into your Facebook and no, I'm not about to start sharing your private Magaluf pictures. Don't worry, those, shall we say, exotic snaps will remain just between you and the other lower-sixth legends.

What I mean is I hope you're learning a thing or two from the small amount of wisdom I have to pass on and that, just like I've done, you can look back on the times when life has given you a good kick in the balls[13] and realise that in the grand scheme of things, none of it really matters. Sure, at the time it was rough but now it's just a story to tell people and hopefully have a good laugh at.

I said at the start that this would be part self-help book, and I hope after all this time we've spent together you've taken away at least a small amount of useful advice. But if not, then I've got just

---

13 Sorry ladies, I don't know what the equivalent danger spot would be for you. The boob? Not sure I could get my leg high enough to kick anyone in the boob, though. Also I'm not a monster.

the thing for you this chapter. You see, I did a bit of research before I started and . . . well, I say research, I popped into Waterstones to get some ideas for what picture I should put on the cover. This meant spending a good amount of time walking back and forth around the non-fiction section. By the way, guys, if like me you sometimes struggle to know the difference between fiction and non-fiction, remember this little trick: fiction means not-real, so non-fiction is not-not-real. This book is not-not-real, aka non-fiction, while *Game of Thrones* is not-real, aka not non-fiction aka fiction. Got it? Simple. Okay then, let's move on.

That morning in Waterstones I realised how popular self-help books were. People like Paul McKenna are totally dominating the place which is mental, because as far as I knew he was just a bloke on telly for a bit who made people go to sleep and wake up thinking they were a chicken or a monkey escaped from the zoo. I thought fair play to you Paul, and bought one of his books to see what the fuss was about and maybe incorporate a bit of his best-selling formula in my own one. I opened it up and expected the whole thing to look just like this:

'Go to sleep. When you wake up, you're going to be a total legend. Now open your eyes. Do you feel like a total legend? Congratulations. Now don't forget to recommend *How to be A Total Legend* to a friend, but don't lend them this copy, make sure they buy a new one.'

I've got to say, though, it wasn't what I expected. Hands up, it was actually pretty good; full of inspirational messages and exercises that mainly involved looking at yourself in the mirror and telling yourself how great you are. Which worked, although Char wasn't too impressed with me taking even more time in the bathroom. One bit that had me in hysterics, though, was this link that came with it to download a track to listen to when you went to bed. So I had a listen and it really freaked me out. First off, he puts on this pan pipes music which is supposed to relax you which but just reminds me of charging round Clintons Cards frantically trying to find a last minute Valentine's card, which is anything but relaxing. Then Paul starts to talk, and oh my God, it's creepy. He drops his voice proper low and exteeeeeeends his wooooooords, I assume trying to sound soothing but it just sounds like he's talking to you in his sex voice. Stop having sex with my ears, Paul!!

Anyway, seeing as the guys publishing this book said I'd be making an audiobook, I thought great, a perfect opportunity to make my own Paul McKenna audio sex tape. Wait, no, nothing like that. If you've only got the normal book (why not get the audiobook as well?), I suggest you lie down and get someone else to read the rest of this chapter out loud for you – just make sure they do so in their deepest, sexiest Paul McKenna voice. Oh, and don't forget the music, that's important. I recommend you hop onto Spotify and find your own pan pipes playlist, and if you don't have access to Spotify, just run over to Clintons Cards and lie on the floor there; they've normally got a sweet pan pipes jam playing over the speakers.

Alternatively, stick a bookmark in and skip to the next chapter. Come back here when you have everything you need.

Still here? Good. Then let's get started. Just lie down, close your eyes, relax and pay attention to the sound of my voice.

Breathe. Breathe long, steady breaths. In – two, three . . . out – two, three. Concentrate on every breath. In – two, three . . . and out – two, three. Relax your entire body. Each time you breathe out, picture yourself getting lighter and lighter. All those stresses you have are melting away. The weight of worry just falling off you.

Did you turn the oven off, by the way? Of course you did. You always do. It's worth asking, though; do you have any idea how many houses burn down each year because people forget to turn the gas off? But you definitely turned it off. You wouldn't be that careless.

Breathe in – two, three . . . and out – two, three . . .

Wait, what's that noise? Did you hear that? Could be a mouse, I suppose. I'm sure everything's fine. It's probably just the wind, in fact. But why would the wind be blowing? Did you leave a window open or something? Great. First you left the gas on and now you've let a burglar in through the window. Good going, genius, no wonder you're so stressed if you go around making mistakes like that.

Breathe in – two, three . . . and out – two, three . . .

You know what, it's making me nervous now. Let's just pause what we're doing and you go and check things out downstairs. Keep the pan pipes music playing, though; the worst thing you can do is let the burglars know you're coming. And take a weapon, too, maybe a razor from the bathroom or a toothbrush to jam into their eye. Hang on, stop. What if there's more than one of them? Better take two toothbrushes. I'll just wait here.

God, I hope you're okay.

What if there is a burglar? There's no way you can actually do any damage with a toothbrush, really, is there?

I mean, I'd hate to have been the one to send someone to their certain de—

You're back! Brilliant. Who was it? It was just the dog, wasn't it? Of course it was. Did you remember to check the oven, too, while you were down there? What do you mean, you didn't? Look, I don't want to have to stop again, it's costing a fortune to rent this sound booth, you know. Get downstairs again and check. I'll wait. I'll just be here checking Instagram.

Wow, this is more difficult than I thought. Paul McKenna makes it look easy.

This studio looks comfy. It's got those squidgy little egg carton sponges all around the walls. They do a pretty good job of blocking out all the sound, I guess. I can't hear a thing. It's weird.

I wonder if a burglar came in here whether anyone would hear me scream.

Are you back now? Good. And the oven was never on, was it? Told you you wouldn't be that stupid. Still, worth it for the peace of mind, right? Okay, lie back down again and relax.

Get back to your slow, steady breathing. In – two, three . . . and out – two, three . . . Make sure you breathe in through your nose and out through your mouth. In through the nose – two, three . . . and out through the mouth – two, three . . .

In – two . . . What's that sound? That whistling? Is that your nose? And out – two, three . . . In – two, three . . . Yes, it is your nose, what have you got up there? You know what, ignore it. Just focus on your breathing instead. In – two, three . . . and out – two, three . . . Feel the air travelling slowly down your windpipe, filling up your lungs. Then feel the air rushing back up your throat and out through your mouth. In through your nose – there's that sound again. Seriously, do you have a cold coming, or something? And out through your mouth – two, three . . . In through your n— Oh God, it's so annoying. It sounds like a mouse crying. Look, let's just stop again. Do whatever it is you need to do to clear whatever it is that's up your nose because we're not going to achieve anything if you don't do something about that.

Finished? Okay, back to it. Unless, wait – what did you do with it? Did you blow it into a tissue? If so, where's that tissue now? And if you didn't, is it like, still on your finger or something? Or somewhere in the bed waiting for you to roll onto and have stuck to your face without you realising? What if you go all tomorrow and no one has the decency to tell you you've been walking around with snot smeared across your cheek? They even have a nickname for you, you know? Boogerboy. That's what they're calling you – Boogerboy. Snot-face Boogerboy. And all because you couldn't be bothered to go to the toilet and use a tissue like a decent human being. Stupid Boogerboy.

Wait. Sorry about that, I got carried away. Really sorry, I'm just really stressed at the moment. Where was I?

Okay, focus on the music. The gentle melody of the pan pipes. Let their rhythm guide your breathing. Picture the wind blowing through the pipes, filling the air with music. Imagine your own body is one big pan pipe. As you breathe in, imagine the air filling your chest with calm, relaxing music, bring your lips close together and let the music play out as you exhale.

It sounds good, doesn't it? Like the musician is there in the room with you. Intimate and soothing. Can you even picture a little Mexican man sat next to you playing away? A private rendition just for you, because you're special, remember that. And you're safe. This little Mexican man will protect you, watching over you as you drift off into a calm, relaxing slumber. His eyes trained on you, not moving away. Wait, that's not relaxing, is it? It's a bit creepy if anything. Okay, forget the Mexican man, he's not there. Start again from the top.

Your mind is full of stresses and we need to remove them one by one. Every time you breathe in, call to mind something that is troubling you. Hold it in your head and picture it in precise detail. Then when you breathe out imagine that stress flowing out from your body and floating away like a helium balloon. Breathe in – two, three . . . picture the stress, focus on it, and breathe out – two, three . . . feel that stress float away. With every exhale your body loses another worry and your body gets lighter. Breathe in again – two, three . . . hold it. Focus. And out – two, three . . .

By the way, I hope you don't think I was being racist when I said the Mexican man was creepy. I didn't mean he was creepy

BECAUSE he was Mexican. Just that it was creepy to have a strange man playing pan pipes next to you while you slept, whatever country he was from. Does that make sense? Because I promise you I'm anything but racist. I mean, I certainly don't hate Mexicans. I love Mexicans. Who doesn't love a burrito, you know, mate? No, I'm not saying that burritos are the only thing Mexicans have going for them. They've given us loads. Like. I mean, there's loads of things. You know. Like. They gave us *pork* burritos, and *steak* burritos, and *barbacoa* ones, and FAJITAS! Yes, Fajitas. That's different. Did they give us Doritos, too? I don't know, I'd have to look that one up. And there's the Mexican wave, too. There you go, I can name loads of good things, so I'm definitely not racist against Mexicans, okay? Ha! In your face!

Wait, what am I doing? This isn't working, is it? I was supposed to be giving you a relaxing, stress-busting experience and I've just ended up talking about Mexicans. God, this is harder than I thought. Fair play to you, McKenna, you win. Keep your millions, or whatever you make from your self-help books, you won't be seeing any competition from me any time soon.

CHAPTER TWENTY-THREE

CHRISTMAS

December is without doubt the best month of the year. I'm one of those people who, as soon as the clock hits midnight on November 30th, I go into full Christmas mode. The decorations come out, the music goes on and *The Muppet's Christmas Carol* gets its first run out on the TV. A lot of people moan about people like us celebrating early but if you ask me, they're just grumpy bastards who can't stay in a good mood for a day let alone a whole month, so they try and ruin it for everyone else. If you're one of those people then kindly pipe down and let the rest of the world get on with enjoying life, and if you're one of us then get out into the streets, put on your best Christmas jumper, puff out your chest and join me in chanting: 'Holidays are coming! Holidays are coming!' . . .

Christmas has always been a big deal for me. Mum and Dad did an amazing job of making it something worth getting excited over, and I want to do my best to recreate that same feeling for my kids. A great Christmas is all about the details. Everything has to be just right, and often if you do one thing differently then it just doesn't feel like Christmas. You ever feel like that, too? If you think I'm being overly dramatic then let me ask, have you ever tried celebrating Christmas at someone else's gaffe instead? It's horrible, isn't it? It's all weird because the routine is different.

'What do you mean, you wait until after lunch to open your presents??' 'What do you mean, you don't link arms and pull crackers all at the same time??' 'What do you mean, you don't get presents for the pets??' 'You're honestly going to sit there and tell me you don't cover your Christmas pudding in brandy and set the thing on fire!??' That's it! Christmas is ruined! I'm going home!

By the way, I'm not saying that I do Christmas the right way and everyone else does it the wrong way. I'm just making the point that a person's way of celebrating is sacred and shouldn't be messed with. So before I go any further, let me talk you through the sacred Christmas routine *I* had growing up.

Christmas Eve was all about Churchill's, the snooker club down the road from Mum and Dad's. It's not there any more, but if you want a sense of what it was like, just picture the club from *Phoenix Nights*; it's exactly the same just with a lot more snooker tables dotted about. It was one big open room with a long bar at one end. The walls were bland and even in the '80s and '90s the decor looked dated. On the walls were framed photos of 'celebrities', none of which I had ever heard of. Any other time of year the place was so dark you couldn't see a thing apart from the various snooker tables lit up from above. But at Christmas, the guys at Churchill's really went to town; the place was filled with flashing lights and tinsel. The kind of over-the-top decorations that these days people would call tacky, but back then Churchill's was like a winter wonderland for kids like me. Every year the atmosphere was amazing. It was the sort of place where the character came from the people that occupied it, and every Christmas Eve it was rammed with the Crascall family: Mum, Dad, me, Amy, grandparents, aunties and uncles. We'd drink all evening and have a real laugh. Over the course of the evening, as more people came into the place they'd join us, and before long our family unit grew and grew until we had the run of the whole place.

When we were done in the club, everyone would come back to Mum and Dad's to continue the party, which always meant an insane number of people cramming inside. They'd all go into the early hours drinking and dancing, but I'd be in bed as soon as I could. Not because I was told to, just because I knew that the sooner I was down, the sooner it would be Christmas.

Here's a question for you reading this, mate: what time would you normally be up on Christmas day? Nine? Ten? Seven, even? Well, not us. When morning finally came around, me and Amy would be up no later than half-five. Knowing we wouldn't be able to touch our presents until Mum and Dad were up, we'd go straight to their room and drag them out of bed. The poor guys had probably only just got to bed and there we were, holding their eyelids open and without fail they'd always have massive hangovers (which Mum would be much better at hiding than Dad).

Mum's first words would always be the same: 'Has he been!? Has he been!?' She'd continue to chant it over and over on our way downstairs. 'Has he been, Arron!? Has he been, Amy!?' In the lounge our presents awaited – we had a sack each with our names clearly written on them, and they'd be positioned in front of Mum and Dad's old '80s fireplace, stuffed with presents. The fireplace was one of them retro-looking ones that looked like someone had smashed apart and tried to put back together again in the dark. On top of it sat one of those clocks that was also a massive boat. I don't know why these were a thing, perhaps mantelpieces were smaller in the '80s so they had to combine all their ornaments with their clocks. Once Mum and Dad were both up, we'd just tear into those gifts one by one. We were seriously spoilt as kids but we had good manners, making sure to be grateful for everything we got. (And *appearing* to be grateful if it was something boring like a pair of socks or a tie I wouldn't wear in a million years). As soon as that mad boat-clock hybrid hit seven, my mum would be in the kitchen, starting on lunch, multitasking while she called the rest of the family, chanting down the phone: 'Has he been? Has he been?' Dad would be with us, cheering as each sheet of wrapping got ripped apart (and at the same time trying his best to keep down last night's ales).

When I was young, the family would flip-flop where we were spending Christmas Day. One year we'd spend all day at home, then the next year we'd be in the car to my Auntie Cagol's. Auntie Cagol always put on a great spread and I had a lot of fun those days, but on those years when you'd received a particularly good gift – a gift too large to take with you in the car, going there for Christmas would be unbearable. No other time was this more true than the Christmas I received my PlayStation One.

On this occasion, I had my suspicions that I was getting one for a while. I'd banged on about it for months; how good the graphics were, how grown-up the games were, how you could play CDs on it! (remember CDs?). Also, Mum and Dad teased me for ages about how I *wouldn't* be getting one; which as we all know is classic parent misdirection. (If they *really* hadn't got me one then they wouldn't have said a thing and hoped I would have just forgotten about the whole thing). When 5 a.m. hit on Christmas morning, I rushed downstairs straight away and there, outside of the sack and lying on the floor was a rectangular box that could only have been one thing: my brand new PlayStation One. Get in, my son!

Amy and I dragged Mum and Dad out of bed just like any other year and I made a beeline for the PlayStation. Sure enough it was exactly what I thought it was, but Mum and Dad made it clear I couldn't plug it in until all the other presents had been opened; which, by the way, took forever! Finally it was time; I was reaching under the TV to plug the PlayStation into the wall when Mum told me to get in the car. I didn't even have a chance to switch the thing on and I was being dragged away to Auntie Cagol's. I wish I could tell you I left with dignity, mate. I'm afraid not. I was kicking and screaming like a two-year-old throwing a tantrum.

When I left I made sure to grab something to remember the PlayStation by. It came with one game, and as it was only the size of a CD, I was able to fit it in the car to take with me. The game was *Ridge Racer* and we were inseparable for every minute I was away. Glance over at me and I'd be on the sofa either reading the instruction manual cover to cover for the thousandth time or just staring hard at the box like I was in some sort of brainwashed trance. If you're thinking, 'Big deal, Arron, you've gone two days without playing a video game', please bear in mind that for me and every other gamer out there, this is the equivalent of Ewan McGregor's epic scene from *Trainspotting* when he tries to come down off heroin. The one with all the screaming, the agony and the baby crawling along the ceiling. The only difference is that unlike Ewan, as soon as I got back I had a hit of speed as quickly as I could. (I'm talking about *Ridge Racer* here, the drugs was just a metaphor).

I'm worried I'm giving Auntie Cagol a bad rap. I really loved spending Christmas over at hers, it's just that on that one particular year, I wanted nothing more than to be at home. When we weren't at Auntie Cagol's, there was one other Christmas tradition we had that these days I really really miss. A family event that sadly hasn't been the same since 2005, which is the year my grandad died. Every Boxing Day until that year, the late, great Fred Crascall would treat the other Crascall men to a trip to watch Dover play football. Remember, without a beer in my hand sport's never been a massive deal to me, but those years, despite being well under the legal drinking age, there really was nothing like lining up on a freezing-cold afternoon alongside Grandad, Dad, Uncle Johnny and my cousin Stephen. There was something about those afternoons that made me feel really grown up. Out there on the terrace

I was one of the men, and I'm sure you'll agree that when you were a kid there was no better feeling than being treated like an adult.

I was very blessed to have people like Fred Crascall in my life. He smelt of brandy and awful aftershave and like all the Crascall men, he was a total joker. We always gave him a load of stick for his old banger, which was this creamy-white Reliant Robin like the sort Del Boy has in *Only Fools and Horses*. That's right, first the mushy pea and now this – what was my family's obsession with rubbish cars? The amount of times I had to force them to drop me off down the road to avoid being spotted, it's a wonder I didn't in fact grow up super-skinny. He was always the first to treat me like a grown-up, and did loads of practical things for me like teach me how to fish. He practically taught me how to drive at the age of ten. I'd sit on his lap in the Reliant Robin and he'd let me turn the steering wheel and work the gears. He'd be in control of the pedals, of course, and rev the car loads so the engine sounded massive.

The annual Dover match is something I'm trying to resurrect for our current Christmas traditions. That time of year is all about family, and it's good to go out and do something special together. Also the kids are probably as grateful as I was to have something else to look forward to once Christmas Day comes to an end. And, because I'm a modern man, I'm getting the girls to come to the games (which is probably something that would have Grandad turning in his grave if he knew!).

After Grandad died, my dad received his walking stick. A pretty boring thing to inherit, you might be thinking, but it was special, this stick, and was a really good way to remember him. Recently Dad accidentally busted the handle off and there, inside the neck of the stick was an emergency bottle of brandy. Fair play to him, man, that's one crafty bloke there. It also explains why he always smelt of brandy.

Okay, before we go any further, there's another important

Christmas rite of passage I need to talk about. One that only happens once in our lifetime. That magical occasion when a special loved one takes you to one side and says . . .

SPOILER WARNING *SPOILER WARNING* *SPOILER WARNING*

Santa isn't real.

END OF SPOILER *END OF SPOILER* *END OF SPOILER*

Everyone remembers the time they found out Santa wasn't real. For me it was Christmas Eve 1991. Before this date, I was utterly convinced he was real and there was nothing you could have said to make me believe he wasn't. Yes, I knew the maths didn't quite add up but my brain kept making excuses for him. Millions of kids across the entire world in one night? I just always assumed it worked because of magic things like time zones (I had no idea what a time zone was).

Can you remember the feeling of trying to sleep on Christmas Eve knowing that at some point in the next few hours, Santa was going to walk past your doorway? In retrospect the thought of a stranger prowling outside your bedroom is the stuff of nightmares, but when you're nine years old it's magical. This Christmas Eve was no different to any other. My brain was refusing to shut down. When you've got half of Dover partying downstairs it's often hard to get to sleep, but on this particular night it was harder than most. The guests must have left well over an hour ago and I was still awake. I kept telling myself that if I shut my eyes hard enough then when I opened them again it would be morning, but it wouldn't work. As I lay there in my tiny bed, I'd stare at the WWF calendar on my wall begging for the next day to hurry up and arrive. But the Big Boss Man would stare right back at me, arms folded, refusing to let time budge. I hated the Big Boss Man. With any luck tomorrow I'd open next year's WWF calendar and he'd be replaced with someone new like The Undertaker.

Children talk about trying to stay awake so they can catch Santa in the act but when I was young, that was never my intention (it's a guaranteed spot on next year's naughty list, surely?). However, on this night I heard a sound that I couldn't ignore. A bang that seemed to shake the entire house. Was that Santa, on the roof? I listened carefully, giving him enough time to climb down the chimney, deposit that Apollo BMX bike I'd been banging on about since Halloween, eat the mince pie I'd picked out for him, then climb back up to the roof and leave. Again, let me reiterate, I wanted him out of there because I had no desire to meet him – I had next year's list to worry about, after all.

Once I was convinced he was gone I climbed out of bed, crept to the edge of my room and tiptoed across the landing, making sure to avoid every creaky floorboard I had memorised. I then began my descent down the stairs with the sort of speed and grace that would give the world's best-trained ninjas a run for their money. (I knew what I was doing, here, I'd seen *Big Trouble in Little China*, and both *Karate Kid* films at least a handful of times each.) I made it downstairs, and was now very much behind enemy lines; there was no turning back. I took two giant, silent steps from the bottom of the stairs to the doorway of the lounge and stood there looking on, expecting to see a bounty of neatly wrapped gifts in front of me. My heart sank. Nothing. All this fannying about getting down the stairs was all for nowt.

'Arron, what are you doing up at this time?' I spun round to see Mum looking on at me, confused. She'd come out from the cupboard under the stairs and there, in her hands, she was wheeling a brand new Apollo BMX. Exactly the same model I had asked for. We stood there looking at each other for ages, neither of us mentioning the obvious. It felt like forever standing there staring, both of us waiting for the other one to do something.

'I just came down for some water,' I said, and sprinted back upstairs – without the water, I should add. I don't reckon I got any sleep that night, I was worrying so much that I'd screwed up. Now that I knew Mum was Santa, did that mean I wouldn't be getting presents ever again? That whole Christmas was awkward, and we carried on as if nothing had happened. Then on Boxing Day, Mum sat me down and talked me through everything. I was gutted. Like I was the last person to be let in on a big elaborate joke. But I wasn't the last, of course – there was still Amy, who Mum made clear wasn't to know. All I wanted to do was run up to her and tell her everything; if I was going to have Christmas spoilt for me, then why should she carry on enjoying it? But my kindness won in the end, and like all older siblings I decided to suck it up and suffer in silence.

My most favourite-ever presents

I think it's pretty fair to say I've been spoilt over Christmas but I've always been very grateful for everything I've received. Even now I don't have to think hard to remember some of my best Christmas presents of all time. I mean, sure mate, I could sit here and list them all for you but that would be boring so allow me instead to declare some of my all-time favourite gifts to the catchy tune of 'The Twelve Days of Christmas'. Feel free to sing along.

On the twelfth day of Christmas my true love gave to me:
Retro Commodore,
Nintendo 64,
Mr Frosty,
A Tamagotchi,
Big Mouth Billy Bass
New Thundercats,
Sega Mega Drive,
NOW TWENTY-FIVE!
PlayStation One,
Two Nerf guns,
That bike wheeled out by Mum,
And Alan Partridge on DVD.

These days there's no denying I still love receiving presents, but I get so much more joy from seeing my kids open theirs; I'll hold my hands up here, I spoil my kids rotten and it's all for selfish reasons. I just love seeing their faces light up every time they open a new gift and I want to see it repeated over and over again. The downside of this generosity is that like most parents, all I wish for now, every single year, is more storage. The biggest cause of stress for me at Christmas is figuring out where to put all their stuff.

Because I have such fond memories of my Christmases as a kid, I feel a lot of pressure to make it just as memorable for my lot, too. Even if Churchill's Snooker Club was still around we wouldn't even have time for a half, that's because Christmas Eves in our house have become a massive operation transforming the gaffe overnight to look like Santa has been. To do this, the average parent would just take a bite out of a mince pie and down a shot of sherry that's been left out for him. Can I just say, though, if Santa were real this strikes me as odd for two reasons. Firstly, if he's taking bites out of everyone's mince pies and not finishing them, isn't he coming across as a little bit ungrateful – especially when he never clears up after himself? 'Oi, Santa, you gonna wash that plate up one of these years?' Secondly, if he's drinking a glass of sherry in every house, he must be driving that sleigh totally off his face! No wonder his cheeks are so red.

Anyway, in our house, rather than settling for just mince pie and sherry, we stage a whole elaborate scene to make it look like Santa's been. By the time we're finished, it looks like a crime scene from an episode of *CSI* (just with a lot more tinsel). Once the kids are in bed, we fake footprints from the fireplace through the lounge to where the presents are left and back again. That involves me walking around in Char's Uggs while she pours talcum powder round my feet. Why she doesn't just wear her Uggs and I do the talcing I don't know, but we've got a system and it's working. After that I proceed to down plenty of beers while constructing a million toys for the kids. If you're a father of young kids, you're guaranteed to spend the hours from ten p.m. on Christmas Eve to three a.m. building stuff. Last year I spent about four hours constructing a trampoline. It was almost time for the family to wake up by the time I was done. I was probably about ten beers in by the time I finally tied the bow on it, which could explain why it took so long, I guess. In a strange sort of passing-the-torch ritual sort of thing, I've now taken over from Dad and spend Christmas Day sat on the sofa with no sleep and a massive hangover.

It's important to remember that Christmas isn't all about presents. Yes, they're a big deal, and are worth getting excited about, but there's something else that's just as important, if not more so. A Christmas tradition of *biblical* proportions, you could say. No, I'm not talking about going to church, I am, of course, talking about the food.

To me, Christmas is one big festival of eating. It starts in November, about the time you do your first shop and the house is full of delicious treats and whenever you step within two metres of that tub of Celebrations someone yells, 'Leave them alone! They're for Christmas!' It then comes full circle and ends on Boxing Day with you reaching for that same tub of Celebrations, deciding you'll eat those remaining Bounties that nobody wanted after all.

For greedy bastards like me, there's no better date in the food calendar than Christmas. It's the only time of the year when it's acceptable to have chocolate, sweets and meat all on the same plate. It also marks the point I complete my full transformation from eating pigs in blankets to becoming one single, giant pig in a blanket. That point, when you're on the sofa, presents opened, drunk on beer and drunk on food, your paper hat firmly planted on your head, sat surrounded by your family, could well be the happiest moment in my life.

This is the point where a lot of families would gather together and watch TV. For me it's always been about *Only Fools and Horses*, but I'd happily make time in my busy eating schedule to watch the *Doctor Who* special with the whole family. Then there's the most important TV of Christmas: The Queen's Speech. I'm sorry to say, Lizzie, that we've never really been a Queen's Speech sort of family (is that treason??). I do love the Queen, though, and I like the idea of her getting on the telly to give people a rousing message of love and support. But I think even she would agree that they're a little bit boring.

If I was King, I wouldn't hold back in my speech I'd tell the country to get real, to be nice and to have fun. It would feel like a slap in the face and a big long hug all at the same time. Yeah, there's lots of shit in the world, but there's a lot of great things too.

I hope you've learned from reading this book that there's more to life than stressing over our everyday gripes. There are lots of things out there in the world for us to have a laugh at and loads of great people out there to have a laugh with.

But sadly for everyone I'm not King, and I've got no Christmas broadcast to tell people what I think. Oh well . . . if only there was a way I could send a message to the population. If only there was some sort of way I could literally get my opinions out of my head and into the hands of the people of Britain and beyond.

Oh, well.

CHAPTER TWENTY-FOUR

THE KING'S SPEECH

By HRH King Crascall the First

Where my subjects at!? People of Britain, make some noise! Everybody put down that Ferrero Rocher and get ready for a truth bomb on the greatest country in the world.

I'm sorry in advance. I'm going to be blunt, but you know what? I need to be, and if anyone's going to be straight-talking it might as well be the one with his sodding face on the coins.

Where to start? Political unrest? Hate? Violence? What's happened to you, Britain? You've had a mad couple of years and at times I'll admit it was exciting, but it's time to get real. You're a mess. Put down that pint, cancel that round of Jäger Bombs and go home, you're drunk. You're going to wake up tomorrow with a massive hangover, but I'm here to tell you that once you push through, things are going to be great again, I promise. We've all had bad days. Just think what it was like for me the day I realised that having a tramp stamp of my own name above my bum wasn't as cool as I originally thought. But now I can have a laugh about it, and you – whatever worry is weighing you down now, you'll be having a laugh at it in a matter of time, I'm sure.

What I want you all to do is go outside, get some fresh air and remember everything that's special about this country. That means looking at the people around you and reminding yourself what's great about your fellow men and women.

Stop focusing on people's faults, and look for the goodness in everyone you meet. Remember, nobody is perfect; I'm the bloody King and there's times even *I* don't wipe my arse properly. (Who am I kidding? As King, I have someone who does that for me.)

You all need a little perspective, so I suggest you each start by opening up Google Maps on your phone and taking a look at where you are. You see the street you're standing on? Put two fingers on that screen and zoom out. You see your town? Your county? Keep zooming. You see how little time it takes before you're looking at the whole country? It's pretty small, dummy, that's why. Realise that. But hey, don't stop there, zoom out some more: Europe, Africa, Asia, America, Australia. Newsflash, people, the entire bloody world is small!

Bear that in mind when you step outside. Take notice of your neighbours and stop pretending like they're so far away. They're not. They're close, they're real and while you look at them they're looking straight back at you. We're all on show, so let's make it the best fucking performance the world has ever seen. Be a good person. No, be a *great* person. Be kind to those less fortunate than you. Be generous, be courteous, be humble, be brilliant.

Because the world is so small it means your opportunities are greater than you think. It means your goals are more achievable than what people tell you they are. And it means you have fewer excuses to not get everything you want out of life.

And let me be clear, I'm not implying that everyone should run out tomorrow and suddenly become an astronaut, a Premiership footballer or the Prime Minister. Everyone's goals are different, and what makes each person happy is different.

My point is that everybody is entitled to happiness and whether that means changing careers, travelling the world, having children, not having children, pwning in *Call of Duty* or (and this is hard to say) playing *Minecraft* for a hundred thousand hours, everyone is entitled to their happiness, and I truly believe that is totally possible so long as you all remember one crucial thing: don't be a dick.

Be nice and have a bloody good laugh out there, people. Now go and eat some chocolate and watch *Die Hard*.

See Ya Later!!!!!

Love, Arron x